WHAT IS CALVINISM?

OR THE

CONFESSION OF FAITH,

IN HARMONY WITH THE BIBLE AND
COMMON SENSE,

IN A SERIES OF

DIALOGUES BETWEEN A PRESBYTERIAN MINISTER
AND A YOUNG CONVERT.

BY THE
REV. WILLIAM D. SMITH, D.D.

PHILADELPHIA:
PRESBYTERIAN BOARD OF PUBLICATION.
No. 1334 CHESTNUT STREET

INTRODUCTION.

There are two causes which exert a powerful influence in rendering unpopular those doctrines usually styled Calvinistic. One of them is radical, and not to be removed by reason or argument. Its seat is in the heart. It consists in a distaste for doctrines which are so humiliating, and therefore repugnant to our depraved nature. The only effectual remedy is the grace of God. When, by the renewal of our minds, we are brought fully and cordially to acquiesce in the Divine government, and to rejoice that the "Lord God Omnipotent reigneth," the *essential elements* of these doctrines will not only form a part of our creed, but become the nourishment of our souls and the source of our purest and most elevated enjoyment.

The other cause alluded to is a misapprehension of what these doctrines really are, as understood by those who believe them. They are often rejected on this ground even by pious men, who, relying upon the representations of uncandid and prejudiced writers or speakers, are made to believe that they are dishonourable to God, and therefore not only to be repudiated, but abhorred. There are not a few, whose religious knowledge is small, that will scarcely listen with patience to Calvinistic preachers, because of the erroneous impression made upon their minds by false and slanderous statements concerning their system of faith. And when they do hear them, and find that no such odious doctrines are preached, they sometimes charge them with hypocrisy in concealing their real sentiments. To remove these prejudices and to enlighten the minds of such, is an important object; and hence a work which states with candor and correctness what these doctrines are, as held by their advocates, which explains, proves, and illustrates them in a kind, lucid, and convincing manner, and thus commends itself to the attention and confidence of its readers, is of great and permanent value. The present volume we regard as such a book; and we most cordially and earnestly recommend it to all candid and sincere inquirers after truth. Upon plain and unsophisticated minds, it can scarcely fail to make a favourable impression. We commend it, also, to the doubting, and even to the prejudiced (if any such are willing to read it), believing that a careful perusal of its contents will produce a beneficial result.

Dr. Smith had served the church as a pastor, as a missionary among the Indians, as an editor of a religious paper, and as a teacher of youth. For two or three years previous to his decease, which occurred in the autumn of 1848, he was a professor in "Anderson's Collegiate Institute" at New Albany, Indiana, where his services were highly appreciated. Only a few days before his death, the honorary degree of D. D. was conferred upon him by the trustees of his *Alma Mater*, Washington College, Pa. As a preacher, he was eminently scriptural. His manners were plain and unaffected; his temper sweet and equable; his conversation agreeable and edifying. He was, in short, "an Israelite, indeed, in whom was no guile." His departure from the world was peaceful and happy. Many tears were shed over his grave, and his memory will be long embalmed in the affections of his numerous friends. Our prayer is that this volume may perpetuate his name and his usefulness to many generations. It is worthy of a place in every Christian family. JAMES WOOD.

INDEX.

WHAT IS CALVINISM?

DIALOGUE I.

INTRODUCTION.

Convert.—I have called this evening to converse with you on a subject, which has of late occupied my mind very much. I have recently, as you are aware, through divine grace, had my mind very seriously exercised on the subject of religion, and now have hopes that I have experienced a gracious change, and have become a child of God—consequently, I have felt desirous of connecting myself with some religious society. As it was through the instrumentality of Presbyterian ministers I was first led to see my lost condition, and ultimately to cast myself on Christ for salvation, I had a preference for that church. But, I have been told, you believe such dreadful doctrines, that I have been led to doubt what would be duty.

Minister.—What are the dreadful doctrines, of our church, which make you hesitate?

Con.—I have been told, you believe that God, by an unchangeable and arbitrary decree, has divided the human family into two classes, elect and reprobate—that the elect, he has, from eternity, decreed to save, let them live as they may. No matter how ungodly, or careless they are, they will all certainly be saved. But the reprobate class are created for the purpose only of eternal damnation, which God has so arbitrarily decreed, that no matter how earnestly and diligently they may seek salvation, they must be lost. These, with a great many other similar doctrines, such as infant damnation, &c., I have been told, are the doctrines of the Presbyterian church, to which I must give my assent before I could be admitted as a member.

Min.—Did any member of our church give you this representation of our faith and practice?

Con.—No, sir. I had them from a neighbour, a member of the Methodist church, who has manifested considerable interest in my case, and expressed his regret that I would even attend a church, where such doctrines are held and taught.

Min.—Did you ever hear such doctrines advanced in our church, by any one?

Con.—No, sir.

Min.—I believe no one has ever heard such doctrines advanced by any Presbyterian; and I have often been surprised at the pertinacity with which such misrepresentations are insisted upon, as being the doctrines of our church. Indeed, I have rarely heard or seen our doctrines stated in their true light, by any of our opponents. They uniformly make some gross misrepresentation of them, such as you mention, and then hold up to odium and ridicule, the creatures of their own misguided, or malignant fancies. It reminds me very forcibly of the infidel, who, in order to show his malignant hatred of the Bible, sewed it up in the skin of an animal, and endeavoured to set his dogs on it. So our doctrines are always dressed up in something that does not belong to them, before any attempt is made to excite odium against them. These misrepresentations, moreover, are often made under circumstances which preclude all excuse on the ground of ignorance. A few weeks ago, in preaching a sermon which involved the doctrine of innate depravity, I took occasion to mention the ground on which we believed in the salvation of infants—that it was not because we believed them holy, and without sin; but, because we believed they were sinful, and would be saved, through the imputed righteousness of Christ. A few days afterwards it was told with a great deal of affected, pious horror, that I had preached the awful doctrine of infant damnation.

Con.—Such things I know have been done, and this led me, at first, to suspect that the representations I had of your doctrines were not true; but my neighbour gave me a book, which professes to give extracts from your standard writers, and the Confession of Faith of your church, in which I find many things to confirm his statements. It was this that staggered me. I could not think that any one would deliberately publish falsehoods; and yet I could hardly believe, that such dreadful doctrines as I find there stated, were in reality the doctrines of your church; and, as I had not access to the writings from which these extracts are said to be taken, and as I wish to make up my mind deliberately on the subject, and act intelligently, I wished to make known to you my difficulties, having confidence that they would be met and treated in a spirit of candour and truth.

Min.—I thank you for your confidence, and hope you will find it has not been misplaced. What is the book that your neighbour gave you, in which you have found those doctrines that you say have been charged upon us?

Con.—It is a volume of "Doctrinal Tracts, published by order of the General Conference" of the Methodist church.

Min.—Are you at liberty to let me examine it?

Con.—I presume so. I will hand it to you, and will call again to-morrow evening.

Min.—I will examine it; and, if I find our doctrines truly stated, I hope I shall be able to show very clearly, that they are the doctrines of the Bible, and of common sense. I wish you to understand, however, that we are not responsible for every expression that may be found in the writings of any individual, though we may approve of his works in the main; and he may be classed among our standard writers. It is only our Confession of Faith that we adopt as a whole, as containing the system of doctrines taught in the Bible.

Con.—Some of the extracts are from the Confession of Faith of your church.

Min.—Very well; all such I am bound to defend, and hope to be able to show you, that the Bible, the Confession of Faith, and common sense, are in perfect accordance with each other.

DIALOGUE II.

MISREPRESENTATIONS OF CALVINISM.

Convert.—Since I saw you, I have been examining, to some extent, the Confession of Faith of your church, and find it corresponds with my own views of doctrine in the main, though I find some things to which I cannot fully subscribe. But, when I look at the Scriptural references, I am forced to believe they are taught in the Bible, and am constrained to leave them, as things I cannot understand. I do not, however, find in it, except in one or two places, anything like the representations I have had of it from others, or the dreadful doctrines quoted in the book I gave you. Have you examined it?

Minister.—I have given it a cursory examination, and have been very much surprised that such misrepresentations, and dishonest and even false quotations, should be put forth and palmed upon the community, under the sanction and by the authority of a church, that has the name of being evangelical. Had it been done by

Universalists, or infidels, it would hardly have been thought worthy of notice; but, when I see it is "published by order of the General Conference" of the Methodist church, I cannot but regret, that that body would sanction, by their authority and influence, the publication and wide circulation of a work, characterized by such an entire want of candour and honesty, and containing so many palpable misstatements.

Con.—Are any of its quotations incorrect?

Min.—There is scarcely a single quotation correct, so far as I have been able to examine it. The first is a quotation from our Confession of Faith, chapter 3, which I find on page 8. It pretends to quote the language of the Confession, but it gives nothing more than a small part of the language, so garbled as to give it an entirely different meaning. The quotation is as follows: "God from all eternity did unchangeably ordain whatsoever comes to pass." Now, let me read the language of the Confession: "God from all eternity did, by the most wise and holy counsel of his own will, freely and unchangeably ordain whatsoever comes to pass; yet so, as thereby neither is God the author of sin; nor is violence offered to the will of the creatures; nor is the liberty or contingency of second causes taken away, but rather established." I will, at another time, endeavour to show you, that this is the doctrine of the Bible, and of common sense. At present, it will be sufficient to say, that, as you perceive, whilst it asserts God's wise and holy purpose respecting "all things," yet it says, also, that he has "so" ordained respecting them, that "he is not the author of sin;" that it does not offer any "violence" or constraint "to the will of the creatures," and in a way that "establishes," rather than takes away, "the liberty, or contingency, of second causes." So, you perceive, that when all these saving clauses are taken away from the language of the Confession, it has a meaning entirely different from that which is intended.

Con.—I perceive the quotation is exceedingly unfair and dishonest.

Min.—On the same page is another, equally unfair, respecting the finally impenitent. It reads thus: "The rest of mankind God was pleased, for the glory of his sovereign power over his creatures, to pass by and ordain them to dishonour and wrath." Now, hear the language of the Confession: "The rest of mankind, God was pleased, according to the unsearchable counsel of his own will, whereby he extendeth or withholdeth mercy as he pleaseth, for the glory of his sovereign power over his creatures, to pass by and ordain them to dishonour and wrath *for their sin*, to the praise of his glorious justice." You perceive that here, also, the language of the Confession is so garbled, as to give it a different meaning altogether. Whilst it asserts that God "passes by" the finally impenitent part of mankind, (that is, he did not determine to save them,) and "ordains them to dishonour and wrath," yet it is "for their sin," and in a manner that will redound "to the praise of his glorious justice." But all this is purposely left out of the quotation, with the design of making it teach the dreadful doctrine of *eternal reprobation*—that God damns man from all eternity, without any reference to his sin, or any reason except his arbitrary decree.

Con.—It is surprising that such things should be published as true, and circulated with so much confidence. The neighbour who gave me the book, said, that I might depend on it as giving, truly, the views of Presbyterians, and that he had the best opportunity of knowing what their views were, as he was brought up under Presbyterian instruction, and had been taught the catechism in his youth.

Min.—As an evidence that he was either unacquainted with the catechism, or with the contents of the book, I will refer you to another quotation, which I find on page 195. It professes to be from the "Assembly's Catechism, chapter 5." Now, as you say you have been looking a little at the Confession of Faith, you have perceived that the catechisms are not divided into chapters; and, where to find the fifth chapter of the Assembly's catechism, we will have to ask "the General Conference," by whose order the book has been published, who should have known, at least, that there *were* chapters in the catechism, before they referred us to one of them. But you will, perhaps, be surprised to learn, that there are not only no chapters in the catechism, but no such language as is quoted. The quotation is as follows: "The almighty power of God extends itself to the first fall, and all other sins of angels and men." Now, there is no such language, or anything like it, anywhere in either of our catechisms, nor is there anything anywhere in the Confession, to afford the least ground for a sentiment so grossly blasphemous as this is made to be, in the connection in which it stands. It is in Tract number 8, entitled, "A Dialogue between a Predestinarian and his Friend," in which the Predestinarian is represented as speaking the language of Calvinists, to prove that God impels men to sin; and, then, this quotation is given, to prove that our catechism teaches, that God's almighty power is exerted in compelling men to sin. On page 194, is another quotation of the same kind, professing to be from the "Assembly's Catechism, chapter 3." But the third chapter of the catechism will be as difficult to find as the fifth.

Con.—But, is there not something, in some other part of the Confession, to give a semblance of truth to the quotation?

Min.—Chapter 5, section 4, of the Confession, thus speaks of God's providence: "The almighty power, unsearchable wisdom, and infinite goodness of God, so far manifest themselves in his providence, that it extendeth itself even to the first fall, and all other sins of angels and men; and that, not by a bare permission, but such as hath joined with it a most wise and powerful bounding, and otherwise ordering and governing them, in a manifold dispensation, to his own holy ends, yet so as the sinfulness thereof proceedeth only from the creature, and not from God, who, being most holy and righteous, neither is, nor can be, the author, or approver of sin."

Now, if this was the passage that was intended by the quotation, it is as dishonest as if they had made the Confession speak the language of Aristotle. The passage, as you perceive, speaks of the "almighty power" of God, as exercised in his universal providence, restraining and governing the sinful actions "of men and angels," and overruling them for good, by a "wise and powerful bounding." And who but an atheist will deny this? It is so plain a doctrine of common sense, that I need hardly stay to reason about it; and it is found on almost every page of the Bible. The wickedness of Satan, in seducing our first parents, as well as their sin, have been, by his "almighty power, unsearchable wisdom and goodness," overruled for good, and "governed to his own holy ends." So, also, the wickedness of Satan in the case of Job, as well as the sins of the betrayer and crucifiers of the Saviour.

Con.—It is certainly a plain dictate of common sense, as well as of the Bible, that God overrules all things, and governs the wicked, as well as the righteous. The Psalmist says, in one place, that he makes the wrath of man to praise him, and the remainder of their wrath he restrains And I was struck with the conciseness and beauty of the language of the Confession, in stating this important doctrine. But, that any one would so garble the passage, as to make it teach the doctrine that God's "almighty power" is exerted in compelling men to sin, is very strange. But, I observed, that the book gives quotations from Calvin, Twisse, Zuinglius, Toplady, and others. Are these quotations equally incorrect?

Min.—I have not examined any of the writers quoted, but Calvin and Toplady. But, I find the quotations from these, are of the same character with those from the Confession of Faith. On page 8, I find a reference to Calvin's Institutes, chapter 21, section 1. Calvin's Institutes consists of four books, and these books are divided into chapters and sections. As the particular book is not referred to in the quotation, I suppose it must be the third that is intended, as none of the others contain twenty-one chapters. I have examined chapter 21, section 1, of book 3, and can find no such language as is quoted, nor anything like it. And, lest there might be a typographical error in the reference, I examined sections 2 and 3, of the same chapter, and section 1 of every other chapter in the whole work, and can find nothing of the kind. On page 97, there is another reference to Calvin's Institutes, chap. 18, sec. 1. As the particular book is not referred to, I have examined chap. 18, and sec. 1, of books 1, 3, and 4, the only ones containing 18 chapters, and can find no language of the kind; and am led to believe, that there is no such language in the whole work. The quotation is as follows: "I say, that by the ordination and will of God, Adam fell. God would have him to fall. Man is blinded by the will and commandment of God. We refer the causes of hardening us to God. The highest, or remote causes of hardening, is the will of God." Book 1st, chap. 18, treats of the manner in which "God uses the agency of the impious, and inclines their minds to execute his judgments, yet without the least stain to his perfect purity"—and, though Calvin uses some expressions that I would prefer to have expressed differently, yet no such language as the quotation, or anything bearing its import, is to be found.

Con.—Could you find none of the quotations referred to?

Min.—On page 194, I find a reference to "Calvin's Institutes, Book 1, chap. 16, sec. 3," in the following language: "Nothing is more absurd than to think anything at all is done but by the ordination of God." In the place cited, there is no such language, or anything like it; but, in sec. 8, I find Calvin speaking of Augustine, who, he says, "shows that men are subject to the providence of God, and governed by it, assuming as a principle, that nothing could be more absurd than for anything to happen independently of the ordination of God, because it would happen at random." I presume this was the passage intended, but you perceive the exceeding unfairness of the quotation. Calvin is speaking of God's providence, which overrules and directs everything, and quotes approvingly the sentiments of Augustine, that nothing happens at random, as if God had no purpose respecting it. But the quotation makes Calvin teach, that God had so ordained all things, that he is the author of sin.

Another quotation, equally unfair, I find on the same page; and here, for the first time, I find the reference correct, though the language is garbled and misrepresented. It is in Book 1, chap. 16, sec. 3. The quotation is as follows: "Every action and motion of every creature, is so governed by the hidden counsel of God, that nothing can come to pass but what was ordained by him." This is made to apply to the actions of men, which would be unfair, even if the language were quoted correctly; for Calvin is speaking of God's providence over his irrational creatures, and arguing against "infidels who transfer the government of the world from God to the stars;" and adds, as encouragement to Christians under God's government, "that in the creatures there is no erratic power, action or motion, but that they are so governed by the secret counsel of God, that nothing can happen but what is subject to his knowledge and decreed by his will." So you perceive, that the language is not only widely different from the quotation, but it is on another subject altogether. On page 176, I find a reference to Toplady's work on Predestination, and the following sentiment given as his: "The sum of all is this: One in twenty, suppose of mankind, are elected; nineteen in twenty are reprobated. The elect shall be saved, do what they will. The reprobate shall be damned, do what they can." Then follow some garbled extracts from Mr. Toplady's work; and an attempt is made, by distorting their meaning, to prove, by inference, that such is his meaning. I need scarcely tell you, that neither Mr. Toplady, nor any other Calvinistic writer, ever penned such a sentiment. It is a gratuitous forgery. The history of it is this: Mr. Toplady published a work on Predestination, which, though it contained unguarded expressions, proved the doctrine so clearly, that Arminians felt it was dangerous to their system. To bring it into disrepute, Mr. John Wesley published a pretended abridgment of it, which was, in fact, only a gross caricature of the work; and yet he put Mr. Toplady's name to it, as if it was the genuine work. To his garbled extracts, he added interpolations of his own, to give them a different meaning, and then closed the whole with the following sentiment: "The sum of all is this: One in twenty, suppose of mankind, are elected; nineteen in twenty are reprobated. The elect shall be saved, do what they will: the reprobate shall be damned, do what they can. Reader, believe this, or be damned. Witness my hand. A. T." Every word of this was a forgery of his own. And yet, he affixes the initials of Mr. Toplady's name, with a "witness my hand," to make his readers believe that it was, in reality, Mr. T.'s language. You will find this, with other facts in the case, stated at large, in Mr. Toplady's letter to Mr. Wesley on the subject, appended to a later edition of his work. Such facts need no comment. The tract in which I find the sentiment again ascribed to Mr. Toplady, was evidently written with a design to screen Mr. Wesley. But such things cannot be excused, in any way, to hide their dishonesty, when the facts are known.

Con.—Is this the character of the quotations generally?

Min.—So far as I have examined, they are generally of this character. I have marked ten or twelve more, which you can examine for yourself, so far as Calvin's Institutes are concerned. I have not, at present, an opportunity of examining the other works quoted; but, from the character of their authors, I must believe they are as grossly misrepresented as Calvin, Toplady, and the Confession of Faith.*

* What I have said of the "Doctrinal Tracts," has occasioned some surprise. Some have even doubted its truth. They think it hardly possible, that the Methodist Church would be guilty of publishing such misrepresentations. If the reader will take the trouble to examine the "Doctrinal Tracts," (the edition published in New York in 1850,) he will find the quotations true to the letter. And he will find, also, that the one half of their enormities has not been exposed. Witness the following, on page 169: "This doctrine (Predestination) represents our Blessed Lord Jesus Christ, the only begotten Son of God the Father, full of grace and truth, as a hypocrite, a

But, be that as it may, we are not responsible for the opinions of either of them, and are therefore not bound to defend them. But, as it respects the Confession of Faith, the case is different. For all its doctrines we are responsible.

Con.—I would be glad if my mind could be relieved of the difficulty under which it labours, respecting some of those doctrines. I am at a loss to reconcile the expressions that "God has foreordained whatsoever comes to pass," and "yet so that he is not the author of sin," &c.

deceiver of the people, a man void of sincerity." And page 170: "It represents the most holy God as worse than the devil, as both more false, more cruel, and more unjust." And again, page 172: "One might say to our adversary, the devil, 'thou fool, why dost thou roar about any longer? Thy lying in wait for souls, is as needless and useless as our preaching. Hearest thou not that God hath taken thy work out of thy hands? And that he doeth it *much* more effectually? * * Thou temptest; He forceth us to be damned. * * * Hearest thou not that God is the devouring lion, the destroyer of souls, the murderer of men?'" &c. And page 173: "O how would the enemy of God and man, rejoice to hear that these things are so! * * * How would he lift up his voice and say, * * * 'Flee from the face of this God, or ye shall utterly perish. * * * Ye cannot flee from an omnipresent Almighty tyrant. * * * Sing, O hell. * * * Let all the sons of hell shout for joy,'" &c. Perhaps I owe an apology to the reader for quoting such language.

Min.—I think them perfectly reconcilable on the plain principles of common sense. But we had perhaps better defer this subject until to-morrow evening.

Con.—I will be glad to embrace the opportunity, at any time you may have leisure.

[It is proper to state that the author of this book is indebted to a sermon of the Rev. A. G. FAIRCHILD, D. D., entitled "The Unpopular Doctrines of the Bible," for many of the arguments and illustrations in the following Dialogues on the "Decrees of God," and "Election."]

DIALOGUE III.

DECREES OF GOD.

Minister.—I think you mentioned, in our last conversation, that one difficulty under which your mind laboured respecting the doctrine of divine decrees, was, that it necessarily made God the author of sin.

Convert.—Yes, sir. I cannot see if God has, "from all eternity, foreordained whatsoever comes to pass," without any exception, how it can be that he is not the author of all evil as well as good.

Min.—The doctrine is not without its difficulties; and, though some of these may be removed by a proper understanding of it, yet when we attempt to follow it out in all its consequences, as with everything else revealed respecting Jehovah, we come to a point at which we are compelled to stop; and, we must, with the docility of children, receive what is told us, though we cannot comprehend it. The doctrine, however, to a certain extent, is very simple and plain All admit that

God is the author and disposer of all things. Nothing takes place except by his agency or permission; or, in other words, nothing can take place, except what he does, or permits to be done. The Bible represents his overruling Providence as extending to all events, however small; the fall of a sparrow, or the loss of a hair. He rules the wicked, as well as the righteous; and his restraining hand is over all in such a way, that it does not infringe upon human liberty. If this were not the case, you perceive, it would be useless for us to pray that God would restrain the wicked in their designs against the Church, or in any other respect; and, indeed, it would close the mouth of prayer almost entirely, to believe God either could not, or did not govern all things, both great and small. Now, though sin is hateful to God, it constantly takes place in his government; and, it is atheism to say, he could not prevent it; for he is not God, if he cannot govern the world. We must, therefore, conclude, he permits it, for reasons unknown to us.

Con.—That is very plain. To say he could not govern and overrule all things, according to his pleasure, would deprive him of his character as infinite; and, to say that he refuses to do it, and leaves the world to manage itself, is not only contrary to the Bible, but is foolishly absurd. But, what connection has this with the doctrine of decrees?

Min.—God, in his providence, fulfills his decrees; or, as the Bible expresses it, "what his hand and counsel determined before to be done"—Acts iv. 28. Hence, our catechism says, that "God executeth his decrees in the works of creation and providence." His providence and decrees are co-extensive; that is, what he does, or permits to be done, in his providence, he always designed to do or permit in his purpose. This is as plain a proposition as the other, and equally consistent with common sense. When he created the world, he of course did it from design; that is, he did not do it by chance, but he designed to make the world just as he did make it. Now, when did he form that design? Did he form the design of creating the world, just at the time it was done, or had he it before? If the design was formed then, he is subject to form new designs, and is therefore changeable; for, it must have been, that he saw some reason for creating a world which he did not see before, or some motive operated which did not before. He must have become more wise, more mighty, or benevolent, or have seen something in a new light, which induced him to adopt the new design of creating the world. But this, you perceive, is blasphemy; for it would make him both finite and changeable. Then, we are driven to the conclusion, that he must have had the design from eternity. Now, the same reasoning, applied to anything he does in creation or providence, will issue in the very same conclusions. If he convert a sinner to-day, he does it from design. But, when did he form the design? Here, you perceive, we run into the same necessity of concluding that the design was eternal, as in the case of the creation of the world. The same is true with regard to what he permits. He permitted our first parents to fall. He permitted Judas to betray the Saviour. He permitted persecution to arise in the Church, under Popery, &c. Did he not know our first parents would fall, when he created them? This, all admit. If, then, he knew they would fall, he determined to permit them; that is, he determined not to prevent them; and, it is in this sense, I use the term permission. Then, if he knew from eternity they would fall, he determined, or decreed, from eternity, to permit them. So with all sin which he sees fit not to prevent. He knew from eternity it would take place, and decreed from eternity to permit it. So we must either admit that what God does or permits to be done, he always designed to do or permit—or deny the perfections of his character.

Con.—But is this permission a decree?

Min.—It is as much a decree as anything else. To decree, is nothing more than to determine beforehand, or to fore-ordain; and, to resolve, or determine to do or permit anything, is to decree it in that sense. The word *decree*, in the sense in which it is used in the Bible, and theology, signifies, "to determine the certainty of a future event, by positive agency or permission." That which is determined to be done, is decreed; and that which is determined to be permitted, is also decreed, when there is power to prevent it; because, when it is known, certainly, that it will be done unless prevented, and there is a determination not to prevent it, it is rendered as certain as if it were decreed to be done by positive agency. In the one case, the event is rendered certain by agency put forth; and, in the other case, it is rendered equally certain by agency withheld. It is an unchangeable decree in both cases. The sins of Judas, and the crucifiers of the Saviour, were as unchangeably decreed, permissively, as the coming of the Saviour into the world was decreed positively. From this you can perceive the consistency of the Confession of Faith with common sense, when it says, that "God from all eternity did, by the most wise and holy counsel of his own will, freely and unchangeably, foreordain whatsoever comes to pass," &c. You perceive, also, that this is clearly reconcilable with the following sentiment, that "he is not the author of sin," &c.

Con.—Still, however, as God is the author of all, and the originator of the plan, does it not still make him the author of sin, in a certain sense?

Min.—His being the author of the plan, does not make him the author of the sin that enters into his plan, though he saw fit not to prevent it. Perhaps I can make this point, and some others connected with it, more plain by an illustration.

Suppose to yourself a neighbour who keeps a distillery or dram shop, which is a nuisance to all around—neighbours collecting, drinking, and fighting on the Sabbath, with consequent misery and distress in families, &c. Suppose, further, that I am endowed with certain foreknowledge, and can see, with absolute certainty, a chain of events, in connection with a plan of operations which I have in view, for the good of that neighbourhood. I see that by preaching there, I will be made the instrument of the conversion, and consequent reformation, of the owner of the distillery, and I therefore determine to go. Now, in so doing, I positively decree the reformation of the man; that is, I determine to do what renders his reformation certain, and I fulfill my decree by positive agency. But, in looking a little further in the chain of events, I discover, with the same absolute certainty, that his drunken customers will be filled with wrath, and much sin will be committed, in venting their malice upon him and me. They will not only curse and blaspheme God and religion, but they will even burn his house, and attempt to burn mine. Now, you perceive, that this evil, which enters into my plan, is not chargeable upon me at all, though I am the author of the plan which, in its operations, I know will produce it. Hence, it is plain, that any intelligent being may set on foot a plan, and carry it out, in which he knows, with absolute certainty, that evil will enter, and yet he is not the author of the evil, or chargeable with it in any way.

Con.—But, if he have the power to prevent the evil, and do not, is he not chargeable with it?

Min.—In the case supposed, if I had power to prevent the evil, yet I might see fit to permit it, and yet not be chargeable with it. Suppose I had power to prevent those wicked men from burning their neighbour's house; yet, in looking a little further in the chain of events, I discover, that if they be permitted, they will take his life; and, I see, moreover, that if his life be spared, he will now be as notorious for good as he was for evil, and will prove a rich blessing to the neighbourhood and society. I, therefore, permit them to do as they please. They, consequently, burn his house, and come with the design of burning mine; but, I have things arranged, to have them arrested and confined in prison, whereby they will be prevented from taking their neighbour's life, which they otherwise would, and he is spared for the great good of the community. Therefore, upon the whole plan, I determine to act; and, in so doing, I positively decree the reformation of that man, and, the consequent good; and, I permissively decree the wicked actions of the others; yet, it is very plain, that I am not, in any way, chargeable with their sins. Now, in one or other of these ways, God "has foreordained whatsoever comes to pass." This, as you know, is the simple language of our catechism, which has been so long and loudly proclaimed as the doctrine of fatality; worse than infidelity; originating in hell, &c.

Con.—The distinction you make between positive and permissive decrees, relieves my mind entirely; and, I do not see how anything else can be believed by any one who believes in the sovereignty of God, as the author and ruler of the universe. And, if this be the doctrine of your church on the subject, it is surprising that such gross misrepresentations of it are so industriously circulated, by professing Christians. They surely do not understand it. Is this view of it given plainly in the Confession of Faith?

Min.—I have never seen it stated in any other work so clearly and concisely, as it is in the Confession of Faith. Chap. 3, sec. 1, which asserts the doctrine of decrees, says expressly, that God has "so" decreed all things, that he is "not the author of sin, nor is violence offered to the will of the creatures, nor is the liberty or contingency of second causes taken away, but rather established." Chapter 5, section 4, thus speaks: "The almighty power, unsearchable wisdom, and infinite goodness of God, so far manifest themselves in his providence, that it extendeth itself to the first fall, and all other sins of men and angels, and that, not by a bare permission, but such as hath joined with it a most wise and powerful bounding, and otherwise ordering and governing of them, in a manifold dispensation, to his own holy ends, yet so as the sinfulness thereof proceedeth only from the creature, and not from God, who, being most holy and righteous, neither is nor can be the author or approver of sin." Here, you perceive, the view I gave is stated in as plain language as could be used. But, further, chap. 6, sec. 1: "Our first parents, being seduced by the subtlety and temptation of Satan, sinned in eating the forbidden fruit. This, their sin, God was pleased, according to his wise and holy counsel, to permit, having purposed to order it for his own glory." So, you perceive, this plain common sense doctrine is the doctrine of the Confession of Faith. It now only remains for me to show, that it is the doctrine of the Bible; for, however reasonable it may appear, if it be not found there, I will give it up.

Con.—I will be glad to avail myself of further instruction on this point, at another time. I have an engagement this evening, that renders it necessary for me to deny myself the pleasure now. Before I leave, however, there is one objection which has arisen in my mind, which I would be glad to have removed. If God permitted evil to come into the world, in order that he might overrule it for good, is not that doing evil that good may come?

Min.—I have not said, nor does either the Confession of Faith, or the Bible say, that God permitted evil in order to overrule it for good. We know nothing but the simple facts, that he permitted it, and has overruled it for good; but, whether that was his reason or not, he has not seen fit to tell us; and, therefore, it is not our place to inquire; and, if men would not wish to be wise above what is written, there would be less controversy and difference of opinion.

DIALOGUE IV.

DECREES OF GOD.

Convert.—In our last conversation, I understood from some of your remarks, that there is an inseparable connection between God's decrees and foreknowledge. Yet, I find the Confession of Faith says, in chapter 3, section 2, that "he hath not decreed anything because he foresaw it as future, or as that which would come to pass upon such conditions."

Minister.—You will observe that the Confession only says, that he did not decree anything because he foresaw it—that is, his foreknowledge is not the ground, or cause of his decrees; still, they are inseparably connected. His decrees are not dependent upon his foreknowledge, nor identical with it; but his foreknowledge is rather dependent upon his decrees, though perfectly distinct from them.

In the case of the distiller, mentioned in our last conversation as an illustration, how could I know certainly that I would go to that neighbourhood to preach, if I had not determined to go? If my purpose to go were in any degree unsettled or undetermined, I could not know certainly that I would go. But, if I had determined to go, then I would know it certainly. So if God knew that he would create the world, it was because he had determined to do it. If his purpose were unsettled, or if he had not come to the determination to do it, he could not know it certainly. But if he had his purpose fixed, then he knew it certainly. It is in this sense that the decrees of God and his foreknowledge are inseparably connected.

Con.—I understand it, I think, now, perfectly, and must confess that the doctrine of decrees, in all its parts, seems to me so reasonable and plain, that I am surprised, more and more, at the virulent opposition which many professors of religion manifest against it. I find, too, from looking at the scriptural references in the Confession of Faith, that it is abundantly sustained by the Bible.

Min.—The passages quoted in the Confession, are but a few of the many with which the Scriptures abound. Indeed, the doctrine is so interwoven through all the promises, calls, threatenings, and instructions of the Bible, that to take it away, would mar the whole. But did you notice the peculiar force of the language of the Bible on this point? One of the passages quoted, is Eph. i. 11—"In whom, (Christ) also we have obtained an inheritance, being predestinated according to the purpose of him who worketh all things after the counsel of his own will." This is stronger language than can be found anywhere in our standards. Here is a "predestination," a "purpose," and a "counsel" of God, "according" to which he "worketh all things." Peter, in his first epistle, i. 20—speaking of Christ, says he was "verily foreordained before the foundation of the world." Now it is admitted on all hands, that God had, in the counsels of eternity, decreed to send the Saviour for the redemption of fallen man; but how could that be, if the fall of man was uncertain? In Acts iv. 27, 28, we read thus: "Of a truth, against thy holy child Jesus, whom thou hast anointed, both Herod and Pontius Pilate, with the Gentiles and people of Israel, were gathered together, to do whatsoever thy hand and thy counsel determined before to be done." Now can any one say, that the death of Christ was an uncertain event in the purpose of God? He knew certainly, that they would assemble to take away his life, and he had decreed to permit it; and thus it was fixed upon as certain, without the smallest possibility of mistake, with the wise and al mighty disposer of all events.

Con.—Then are we to conclude that Judas and his accomplices could not have acted otherwise?

Min.—That does not necessarily follow from the absolute certainty of their course. They could have acted otherwise, if they would. A man has power to do that which it is absolutely certain he will not do, and to refrain from doing that which it is absolutely certain he will do. Had the Saviour called "twelve legions of angels," which he said he could have done, and overcome the band that came against him with Judas, or forcibly prevented them in any other way; or if he had impelled them against their will to do as they did, they could not have acted freely. But he left them to fulfil his purpose, in doing as their wicked inclinations prompted them. Hence, Peter charges them with the crime, whilst at the same time he declares that they acted according to the purpose of God. Acts ii. 23—"Him being delivered by the determinate counsel and foreknowledge of God, ye have taken, and by wicked hands have crucified and slain." From this you can perceive that the Confession of Faith speaks the language of the

Bible and of common sense, when it says, that God has so decreed all things, that "no violence is offered to the will of the creatures, nor is the liberty or contingency of second causes taken away, but rather established."

Con.—But if God thus brings good out of evil, and the wicked actions of men are all thus overruled for his glory, why are wicked men punished?

Min.—This is the very objection that the apostle meets, in Rom. iii. 5—"If our unrighteousness commend the righteousness of God, what shall we say? Is God unrighteous who taketh vengeance? (I speak as a man)"—that is, he speaks the language of a common objection, which men might be likely to make, and no doubt did make, then as well as now. But how does he answer it? "God forbid; for, then how shall God judge the world?" The same objection he meets in the 9th chapter and 19th verse: "Thou wilt then say unto me, Why doth he yet find fault; for who hath resisted his will?" And what is his answer? "Nay, but O man, who art thou that repliest against God?" This would be sufficient; but I may add, that an action being overruled for good, cannot, in the smallest degree, lessen its criminality. In the case I have already supposed, my determination to overrule for good the wickedness of those men in burning their neighbour's house, and attempting to burn mine, could not, in any degree, lessen the criminality of their actions. So you perceive, that God can still "judge the world" in righteousness, as Paul asserts, though he overrules sin to his own glory, and for a greater good.

There are hundreds of other passages in the Bible equally as plain as those I have mentioned. Isa. xlvi. 10—"I am God, and there is none like me, declaring the end from the beginning, and from ancient times the things that are not yet done, saying, my counsel shall stand, and I will do all my pleasure." Paul, in Acts xvii. 26, says, God "hath made of one blood all nations of men, for to dwell on all the face of the earth, and hath determined the times before appointed, and the bounds of their habitation." I shall cite but one passage more, though I might produce a hundred. Joseph's brethren were, like the crucifiers of the Saviour, very guilty in selling their brother into Egypt; but he tells them plainly, Gen. l. 20—"As for you, ye meant it for evil against me, but God meant it unto good, to bring to pass, as it is this day, to save much people alive." Now can anything be plainer, than that God intentionally permitted the selling of Joseph for important reasons, and had decreed so to do, as well as to direct his future course? Now I would ask any candid man, whether the Confession of Faith pushes the doctrine of decrees further than the Bible?—or, whether common sense can find any other system of doctrine, consistent with the character of God?

Con.—My mind is perfectly satisfied that the doctrine of the Confession is both reasonable and scriptural. But I have a difficulty still, with regard to some of its consequences. If all things are so certainly arranged in the purposes of God, what encouragement have we to pray?

Min.—We have infinitely more encouragement to pray, than if events depended upon creatures, or were suspended in uncertainty. God has so arranged all events, that every effectual fervent prayer of the righteous shall be fulfilled, and that without resorting to miracle, or interfering with his other purposes. But take away the doctrine, and we have no encouragement to pray, that I can conceive of. You ask God to convert a sinner, but if the matter be not in his hands, and is left to chance, or the sinner's own natural inclinations, you pray in vain. God cannot interfere for fear of destroying free agency. Thus you perceive, that if God be not the sovereign disposer of all events, the mouth of prayer is closed. But if it be a part of his plan, certainly to answer every prayer of faith, then we can come to him with confidence and great encouragement.

Con.—But does it not discourage the use of means?

Min.—In the illustration I gave of the distiller, did my determinations and arrangements in my plan, discourage the use of the means in carrying it out? It embraced all the means of its accomplishment; and the arrangements of the plan were the ground of encouragement for the use of the means. So of God's plan. It embraces all the means of its accomplishment; and when we engage in his service, in the use of his prescribed means, we have the great encouragement of knowing that it is by these he has determined to accomplish his great work.

Con.—It is to be regretted that this doctrine is by so many misunderstood. Would it not have been better for the framers of the Confession of Faith, to have been a little more guarded, and not to have used language that was so liable to be misunderstood and perverted?

Min.—I know not what they could have done more than they have, without departing from Scripture truth. The Confession is easily understood by any one who wishes to understand it. We may as well say, why did not the writers of the Bible use other language? There are hundreds of passages in the Bible just as strong as any used in the Confession. Why did Paul say, "predestinated according to the purpose of him who worketh all things?" &c. Why did he not leave out the whole of the first chapter to the Ephesians, and the eighth and ninth to the Romans? Indeed I believe if the framers of the Confession had taken verbatim some passages of Scripture, it could not have lessened the opposition. Jude says, there were certain men "who were before, of old, ordained to this condemnation." Now if the framers of the Confession had taken that language as it stands, without inserting the words "for their sin," what would our enemies have said?

Con.—I believe it is best to follow the Bible, regardless of the opinions of men; and I believe the truth will ultimately commend itself to all intelligent minds. I would be glad to have some further conversation with you on some other doctrines which I find it difficult to understand, if it would not be trespassing too much upon your time.

Min.—I will be glad to give you all the information I can, and will be at leisure to-morrow evening, when we will take up the doctrine of election, as it is intimately connected with the doctrine of decrees.

DIALOGUE V.

ELECTION.

Convert.—Since our last conversation, I have been examining the Confession of Faith, and have been not a little surprised that I cannot find the terms *reprobate*, and *reprobation*, anywhere used. I thought they were used in contradistinction to the terms *elect* and *election*.

Minister.—They are not used in our standards, I believe, anywhere, though uniformly charged upon us, as an epithet by which to excite odium. I have been the more surprised at this, because they are Scripture terms; and I would have no objection to use them in the sense in which the Bible uses them. They mean, ***not approved***, or chosen; and if in this sense applied to the finally impenitent, their use would be proper. But the enemies of the doctrine of election have coined a new meaning for the words, and then charge us with using them, with their meaning. The doctrinal tracts of the Methodist church, which we examined some time ago, ring their changes upon "election and reprobation," as if scarcely anything else were in our standards; whereas, reprobation, in the sense in which they use it, is neither part nor consequence of the doctrine of election.

Con.—The idea I have had of the common meaning of the term reprobation, is, that God made a part of mankind merely to damn them; and that he has, by his decree respecting them, made it impossible for them to be saved, let them do what they may; and that this is a necessary consequence of the doctrine of election, and so necessarily connected with it, that they must stand or fall together.

Min.—I know this is the common misrepresentation, but such sentiments are nowhere to be found in our Confession of Faith, or in any of our standard writers; and only exist in the imaginations and writings of errorists, who scarcely ever oppose the truth without misrepresentation. Election has nothing to do with the damnation of a single sinner. It is God's purpose of love and mercy, embracing in itself the means and agencies for carrying it out. It embraces no decree or purpose that hinders any one from coming to Christ and being saved, if they would. There is nothing that hinders their salvation but their own aversion to holiness, and their love of sin; and it is for this, that God has purposed to damn them

Con.—What then is the doctrine of election, as held by the Presbyterian church?

Min.—The best definition I can give of it, is contained in the answer to the 30th question in our Larger Catechism: "God doth not leave all men to perish in the estate of sin and misery, into which they fell by the breach of the first covenant, commonly called the covenant of works; but of his mere love and mercy, delivereth his elect out of it, and bringeth them into an estate of salvation, by the second covenant, commonly called the covenant of grace." Now one simple question will determine the truth of this, on the plain principles of common sense. Does God save all men out of their estate of sin and misery, or does he leave some to perish in their sin, as they choose? If he saves all men "through the sanctification of the Spirit and belief of the truth," then the doctrine of election is not true; but if he does not, then it is true.

Con.—It is very plain, that he does not save all men; but does he not offer salvation to all men?

Min.—Certainly. But do you suppose

that nothing more is necessary for salvation than to offer it?

Con.—By no means. I believe if God would leave men with a mere offer of salvation, not one would ever accept of it. At least I judge so from my own experience. I fully believe, if he had not come with the influences of his Spirit, I should have listened carelessly to the calls of the Gospel, until death would have sealed my doom for ever; and I feel that I cannot be too thankful for his unspeakable mercy.

Min.—You believe then, that salvation is entirely of God; or as the apostle expresses it, he is "the author and finisher of our faith;" and that he has done a work in this respect for you, which he has not done for your unconverted neighbour. But do you suppose it was on account of anything naturally good in yourself, that he made the difference?

Con.—I can take no praise to myself. I was running the same course with my wicked companions; and in some respects I believe I was the most wicked of all. I know and feel that it is all of grace, and can truly say, it is "by the grace of God I am what I am."

Min.—Your experience in this respect, corresponds with the language of Scripture, 1st Cor. iv. 7—"Who maketh thee to differ from another; and what hast thou, that thou didst not receive?" Eph. ii. 1—"You hath he quickened, who were dead in trespasses and sins." John i. 13—"Which were born, not of blood, nor of the will of the flesh, nor of the will of man, but of God." Tit. iii. 5—"Not by works of righteousness which we have done, but according to his mercy he saved us, by the washing of regeneration, and the renewing of the Holy Ghost." Indeed the Bible everywhere ascribes salvation entirely to God; and I have never yet been able to find a true Christian who felt he had any ground of boasting, as being in any sense, or in any degree, the author of his own regeneration. But as you ascribe the work entirely to God, do you suppose he intended your regeneration and conversion, when he came in mercy by his Spirit; or was it accidentally done, without any gracious design towards you?

Con.—I can hardly suppose you serious in asking such a question.

Min.—It does imply an absurdity. A man who acts without design, or purpose, is accounted foolish; and it would be both absurd and impious, to impute anything of the kind to God. But I proposed the question preparatory to another. If God acted with a gracious design in thus changing your heart, when did he form that design? Do you suppose he conceived a gracious purpose towards you at the time, or had he it previously? And if he had it previously, when was it first formed?

Con.—It must have been eternal, for he cannot have any new designs. With him there cannot be any succession of time. He is "from everlasting to everlasting;" and as his existence is eternal, and "his understanding infinite," all his designs and purposes must be eternal. And when I think of his "gracious thoughts" towards me, and attempt to trace them to their fountain, I find myself lost in eternity.

Min.—You have now expressed everything that is intended and embraced in the doctrine of election. It is simply grace traced to its eternal source. It is the design or purpose of God, to accomplish that work of grace in the heart, which believers experience in regeneration, and to carry it on to perfection and glory. Now the simple question is, Did he purpose to accomplish this work of grace in the hearts of all men? This no man of common sense can believe. So you perceive, we must either deny the doctrine of regeneration and sanctification by grace, or admit the doctrine of election. Those who pretend to believe that salvation is entirely by the grace of God, and yet deny the doctrine of election, can lay but few claims either to consistency, or common sense.

Con.—But does not the believer do something in his own conversion?

Min.—The action of the mind in believing and turning to God, is the believer's own work; that is, he believes. God does not believe for him. But this is the fruit of regeneration; and they are so intimately and inseparably connected that persons do not always distinguish between them. They are, however, clearly distinct. Breathing is the result of life, and always inseparably connected with it. A person must live in order to breathe, yet breathing is the operation of life, not life itself. So in spiritual life. Regeneration is the giving of life; and holy exercises are the operations or action of a "quickened" soul. Your own experience will perhaps be the best illustration of the fact. Though convinced of sin, and dreading its consequences, you felt a strong disinclination to give yourself to God, on the terms of the Gospel; but you were afterwards brought to see its beauty, and its perfect adaptedness to your case. It was the same Gospel, and the same Saviour, who had been offered before, but you seemed to view them in a new light. You, in short, felt your views of God and religion changed, in a way that led you to desire and seek what you formerly disliked and slighted. Now it is this change of views and feelings, that is called regeneration, and is the work of God; and the exercises of love, faith, and hope, and the action of giving yourself to God, consequent upon your change of feelings, is conversion. Now it is admitted on all hands, that you acted freely, and felt that you were exercising and doing those things yourself; but the question is, Did you change your own feelings? This you have said, and the Bible everywhere declares, is the work of God. In doing it he accomplished a gracious design, which he had toward you from eternity; and that gracious design was your election. Hence it is sometimes called personal election, because God has the same gracious design toward each individual whom he calls.

Con.—It is surely a doctrine that is calculated to excite gratitude in the heart of a Christian; but does it not show partiality in God, in doing more for some than others?

Min.—God distinguishes, it is true, but he is not partial; for partiality means a preferring one before another, without sufficient reasons, or overlooking just claims. If any of the human family could claim anything at the hand of God, there would be cause of complaint, that some were passed by in his purpose of mercy. But when all equally deserve hell, if he see fit to save some, for a display of his mercy, and leave others to the fate they choose, for a display of his justice, though the former have great ground of gratitude, the others have no cause of complaint.

Suppose the monarch of some mighty empire hears that some province of his dominions has rebelled. Having no pleasure in their death, he sends them an offer of pardon upon consistent terms, and they all refuse to accept it. Still inclined to mercy, he sends out ambassadors, who use every entreaty with the rebels, but in vain. They call their monarch a tyrant, and persist in their wicked rebellion. The compassionate monarch, still unwilling to give them up, goes among them himself, and by his own personal influence, prevails on a greater part of them to accept his proposals of pardon. But as such signal obstinacy ought not to go unpunished, he executes the sentence of the law on the rest. Thus the greater part are reconciled, and the rest are punished. Now who could accuse the monarch of partiality, or blame his course?

But vary the case a little. Suppose this monarch has foreknowledge, and can clearly foresee the rebellion long before it takes place. He reasons with himself thus: "I see that some years hence, part of my kingdom will rebel. Well, I will send them a proposal of pardon. But I know they will all reject it. I will then send special messengers to explain to them their danger, and the honourable manner in which I wish to save them, and to use every entreaty to bring them back to their allegiance. But I see they will reject all. I will then go myself, and prevail on the greater part of them to accept my offer, and will punish the remainder as ensamples to my whole empire. But seeing that my proclamation and my messengers will effect nothing, shall I omit to send them? No, I will send them to convince all of my sincerity in offering pardon and mercy; to show what obstinacy existed in the hearts of the rebels; and to convince all of the wisdom, justice, and mercy of my proceedings."

Now can we find any more reason to blame the monarch, because his determinations were formed previously to the rebellion? Can we condemn him for taking the course he ought to have taken, if his purposes had not been formed until the time? Was he partial in determining to make a public example of some of the rejecters of his mercy? Can any one say that his determination to save some, wronged the others? Did his decree to save some, fix the condition of the others, so that it was impossible for them to accept his offer of pardon? They fixed their condition themselves. They were "ordained to wrath and dishonour for their sins." But will any one blame him for not constraining all to accept his offer? This were to allow him no room for the exercise of discretion. Or will any one say he ought not to have used his influence to persuade any, but left all alike? Then there would have been no objects upon whom to exercise mercy.

Now though we cannot find an illustration that will exactly, in all points, meet the case, yet I have, I believe, in this, exhibited our view of election in every material point, and you can easily make the application of it in your own mind to God, as the sovereign of the universe, and this world a rebellious province. God in infinite mercy, has offered pardon to the rebels of Adam's race, through his Son. His language is, "Whosoever will, let him come." But all refuse; and if left to themselves, every individual of mankind will reject the offer, and everlastingly perish. Christ would have died in vain, and there could be no trophies of his mercy. But God determined that this should not be the case. He sends his Spirit, and sweetly constrains them to yield, in a manner that will for ever redound to the praise of his mercy and grace. What proportion of the human family he has included in his purpose of mercy, we are not informed; but, in view of the future days of prosperity promised to the church, it may be inferred that the greater part will, at last, be found among the number of the elect of God. But although the number is unknown to us, it is "certain" and "definite" with God; so that he cannot be disappointed, either in finding among them one whom he did not expect, or in losing one he purposed to save. This is what our Confession of Faith means, and all it means, in saying that the number is so "certain and definite, that it cannot be increased or diminished."

I have now, I think, shown you that the doctrine of election is in every point, a plain dictate of common sense. I wish also to show you that it must be true, from the character of God and the Bible. But our conversation has been sufficiently protracted at this time. Call when you have leisure, and we will pursue the subject further, in the light of God's word.

DIALOGUE VI.

ELECTION.

Convert.—Since our last conversation, I have been reflecting on the views you presented, and am constrained to acknowledge, that I can find no other doctrine consistent with facts, the character of God, and the Bible. It is a fact that must be conceded, that God is the author of regeneration; and this once conceded, the doctrine of election must be true, or we at once deny his character as infinite. But still there are some consequences of the doctrine, which seem to me irreconcilable with God's goodness and sincerity, in offering pardon to sinners. Does it not render it necessary that some must be lost, and some must be saved?

Minister.—You fail to distinguish between necessity and certainty. If you were to say, it renders it certain that some will be lost, and some will be saved, then you have the true issue; but this, you perceive, alters the case materially. There is no necessity placed upon the impenitent to refuse the offers of the Gospel, though God knows certainly they will. But even that certainty does not flow from the doctrine of election. Take away the doctrine, and see if the case will be any better. Will any be saved without election, that will not be saved with it? If you take away God's special purpose to save, every sinner of Adam's race will most certainly perish.

Con.—But still it seems that God cannot be sincere in offering salvation to all men, when it is certain that some will not accept it.

Min.—If he had formed no purpose to save any, and offered salvation to all, knowing they would refuse, could he be sincere?

Con.—Certainly; for if they would accept, they would be saved. Besides, he might offer, knowing certainly they would refuse, to show his willingness to save, and the justice of their condemnation.

Min.—You have now answered the objection; for God's purpose to save some, does not affect, in any point, the light in which he stands to the rest, or the relation in which they stand to him. They are left just as they were; and still, if they would accept his offer, they would infallibly be saved; and it is just as much their duty to repent and be saved, as if he had elected none.

Con.—But will the doctrine not discourage the use of means, and making exertions to obtain salvation ?

Min.—To whom can it be discouraging ? Surely not to ministers of the Gospel. When Paul was preaching at Corinth, he was discouraged until God preached to him the doctrine of election. In the midst of his discouragement, how cheering it must have been to be told of God, "Be not afraid, but speak, * * for I have much people in this city."—Acts xviii. 10. Now here we have election from the mouth of God; and what could be more encouraging than to be thus informed, that God intended to convert a number of that wicked city through the instrumentality of his preaching? Now you will observe, God did not tell Paul he had all the city, nor how many. It was enough for Paul to know he had some. He could then go forward, confident of success. Take from me the doctrine of election, and I have not the least hope of success. But when I know that God has determined to save a vast number of the human family in every age, "by the foolishness of preaching," I can go forward in the use of his appointed means, with confident hope

Neither can it be discouraging to sinners. It is the sinner's only hope. Take it away, and despair must shroud the whole race of Adam. But the sinner can now come to God, trusting in his special purpose of mercy, feeling that his help is laid upon one who is mighty to save, and who will infallibly save every one who comes to him through Christ. I know the doctrine sometimes makes careless sinners uneasy, and wicked men uniformly hate it. But what does that amount to? Simply this. They refuse mercy, and wickedly reject God's grace; and knowing that they cannot be saved in sin, and being unwilling to repent, they hate the whole system of grace. But if any one truly desires salvation, and wishes to turn from sin, he finds in the doctrine of election the richest encouragement. Would it not be encouraging to the people of Corinth, to know that God had purposed to convert a number of them, and make them trophies of the cross? But is the doctrine discouraging to the praying Christian? He acknowledges the truth of it every time he prays that God would convert sinners, and build up his Church. And it is the fact, that God has promised to give this world to his Son, and gather the vast multitude of his elect from every nation, that is his only encouragement to pray. I have, indeed, sometimes wondered what encouragement those have to pray, who deny the doctrine. If it be not true that the work is God's, and he has purposed to carry it on, why need any one pray? If the work be left to the decisions of sinners, or to chance, the proper course would be to pray to those who have the work to do. It is foolishly absurd, as well as impious, to deny that the work is God's, and then pray that he would do it. So you perceive it is the denial of the doctrine, that discourages prayer. But what encouragement it affords, to know that God has purposed to carry on this glorious work, until the blessed religion of Jesus shall triumph over the whole world, and has declared, too, that it will be done, in answer to the earnest prayers of his people.

Con.—I see much depends upon a right understanding of the doctrine. But still, is it not calculated to do harm?

Min.—How can it do harm? We have seen that it contains the only ground of hope to the minister as well as the sinner. Who was a more zealous advocate for the doctrine than Paul? There is no modern writer who states the doctrine so plainly, or in so forcible language; and yet who was more zealous and indefatigable in labours? And the reason is plain. He knew that God had determined to save a great many in the world, and had placed the instrumentality in his hands. This, with love to his Master, constituted the glorious motive that actuated him in all his labours. Can it do harm for a minister to believe that God, the Father, has promised the Saviour "a seed," which shall surely be gathered, as the glorious reward of his sufferings? and that his is the important work, so far as instrumentality is concerned, of gathering this promised seed to the Saviour? Could there be any higher motive placed before the mind of a true lover of the Lord Jesus Christ? Or can it do harm to preach this doctrine as a motive to Christian effort, or as an inducement for sinners to believe? When a sinner is told that there is nothing on the part of God to keep him away; that there is nothing but his own unwillingness and hatred of God, that stands in the way of his acceptance; and that if he will only give himself to God, on the terms of the Gospel, he will be among those whom God has purposed to save; he has the greatest encouragement that can be given, to look to God for grace, and pray that he may be included in the number of his chosen.

But I grant there is one way in which these doctrines are the occasion of harm. When our enemies misrepresent them, and endeavour to make people believe that we make God the author of sin; that we deny free agency, and the use of means; and loudly proclaim that our doctrine "came from hell, and leads to hell;" and that, "according to our belief, sinners may rest secure, the elect must be saved, and the rest must be damned, do what they may," &c., people will take occasion to say, "if so large, respectable, and upright a class of Christians, believe a doctrine which is pronounced 'worse than infidelity,' there is no truth in religion." In this way the doctrine is the occasion of much harm. But because others wickedly "turn the truth of God into a lie," must we, therefore, give it up? We may as well say that Christ should not have preached concerning "his kingdom," because he was wickedly misrepresented as claiming an earthly crown.

Con.—I know such assertions are often made; and I could not but wonder that such awful doctrines were believed by a class of Christians that seemed so generally pious and upright in their deportment, and at the same time so zealous in the cause of Christ. I found them as a body, generally, the most liberal in sustaining the cause of benevolence, and making at least full as many sacrifices and efforts for the spread of the Gospel, as any others.

Min.—Let us now attend to some direct proofs of the doctrine of election; and I would remark that it must be true, in the first place, from the character of God and his promises.

Laying aside the thousand other promises he has made on this subject to his church and people, I will only mention the reward promised to the Saviour. Would Christ suffer and die on an uncertainty? Would the Father subject his Son to all the infinite load of wrath which he bore for sinners, without any certain prospect of an adequate result? And if he himself had not made it certain, how could it be certain? If it were placed in any other hands but his, it could not be certain. Let us for a moment suppose that God has not positively determined to bring any one to Christ; and where is the certainty that any will come?

Con.—In that case it would be certain that none would come.

Min.—Then you perceive we are at once driven to the conclusion that he determined to "make them willing," or there could be no certainty that the Saviour should "see of the travail of his soul, and be satisfied." We might reason in the same way respecting all the attributes of God. It is inconsistent with any one of them to deny his special purpose of mercy. But enough has been said, in the light of reason. Let us examine the Bible, and see if it teaches the doctrine; for however reasonable it may appear, if it be not plainly taught there, we must give it up. Eph. i. 4—"According as he hath chosen us in him before the foundation of the world, that we should be holy and without blame, before him, in love;" and that his meaning might be the more plain, he adds in the 5th verse, "Having predestinated us unto the adoption of children, by Jesus Christ, to himself, according to the good pleasure of his will." And in the 11th verse of the same chapter, he says, "In whom also we have obtained an inheritance, being predestinated according to the purpose of him who worketh all things after the counsel of his own will." Does not this look like the doctrine of election? But again, Rom. viii. 28—"We know that all things work together for good, to them that love God; to them who are the called, according to his purpose." "For, whom he did foreknow, he also did predestinate to be conformed to the image of his Son. * * Moreover, whom he did predestinate, them he also called, and whom he called, them he also justified, and whom he justified, them he also glorified." Now if the doctrine of election be not true, we may safely challenge any man to tell us what the apostle means by such language. But in 2 Thess. ii. 11—13, he uses still stronger language: "And for this cause, God shall send them strong delusion that they should believe a lie, that they all might be damned, who believed not the truth, but had pleasure in unrighteousness." Is the language of our Confession stronger than this, when it says, they were "ordained to wrath and dishonour for their sins." People may call this reprobation, or give it any other opprobrious epithet, and say, "it originated in hell," &c.; but there it is in the language of Paul, much more strongly expressed than in our Confession. But in the very next verse, we have the doctrine of election, expressed in language equally strong: "But we are bound to give thanks alway to God, for you, brethren, beloved of the Lord, because God hath, from the beginning, chosen you to salvation, through sanctification of the Spirit and belief of the truth." He expresses the same sentiment in language equally explicit, in his

2d epistle to Timothy, i. 9—"God hath saved us, and called us with an holy calling, not according to our works, but according to his own purpose and grace, which was given us in Christ Jesus, before the world began." Such is the language of Paul on the doctrine of election; and any person is at liberty to weigh our Confession of Faith in this balance.

But let us see what our Saviour himself says on this point. John vi. 36—"All that the Father giveth me shall come to me, and him that cometh to me I will in no wise cast out." Here he first states God's special purpose of mercy, in giving him a seed to serve him, and the certainty of their coming; and then adds the encouragement it affords for sinners to believe. He, it seems, did not think the doctrine discouraging. Those that the "Father gave him," he calls his sheep—John x. 27—"My sheep hear my voice, and I know them, and they follow me, and I give unto them eternal life, and they shall never perish, neither shall any pluck them out of my hands. My Father, who gave them me, is greater than all, and none is able to pluck them out of my Father's hands." And in allusion to the Gentiles, who had not yet had the Gospel preached to them, he says, in the 16th verse, "Other sheep I have, which are not of this fold; them also I must bring, and they shall hear my voice." If this does not express a special purpose of mercy towards all those that shall be eventually gathered in, language has no meaning.

But finally, he tells us of a day in which he will preach the doctrine to the assembled universe, amidst the awful grandeur of the judgment, and with a voice more awfully impressive than ten thousand thunders. Matt. xxiv. 31—"And he shall send his angels, with a great sound of a trumpet, and they shall gather together his elect from the four winds." And in the 25th chapter, and 34th verse, he tells us how he will address them: "Come ye blessed of my Father, inherit the kingdom prepared for you from the foundation of the world." And to the others who, as Paul expresses it, "had pleasure in unrighteousness," he will say, "Depart ye cursed into everlasting fire, prepared for the devil and his angels." Thus his purpose of mercy will be fulfilled in a manner worthy of it, and of himself; and his purpose of judgment, too, respecting the finally impenitent, will be fulfilled in a manner that will for ever vindicate him from the charge of partiality.

Con.—It will certainly be a grand and

glorious winding up of a scheme, equally grand and glorious; and I think it will then be acknowledged that the whole plan was laid in eternal and infinite wisdom and love, and executed in infinite grace and glory. I begin to see now the beauty and consistency of the Calvinistic scheme, because it is the scheme of the Bible. Those doctrines I find are justly styled the "doctrines of grace," and I would like to examine with you some more of the prominent points of this scheme, if I have not already consumed too much of your time.

Min.—I consider my time well spent in vindicating the truth from the aspersions of its enemies. I shall be pleased at any time to examine with you any other doctrine of our Confession, about which you have any difficulty.

Con.—There are some things about the doctrine of total depravity, that I cannot fully understand. I have no doubt as to the fact; but how we are held responsible for Adam's sin, presents a difficulty to my mind.

Min.—We will take up that subject at our next interview.

DIALOGUE VII.

ORIGINAL SIN.

Minister.—In our last conversation you mentioned a difficulty under which your mind laboured, respecting the doctrine of hereditary depravity; but I think you stated that you had no difficulty as to the fact that all mankind are depraved.

Convert.—Judging from the exhibitions of human nature, as they are seen on the general face of society, I do not see how any one can deny the fact. Looking at these exhibitions, under any circumstances yet found in the world, it seems to me that any reflecting mind must be convinced that mankind are, by nature, "wholly inclined to sin," as I find it expressed in the Confession of Faith.

Min.—Your sentiments accord with the language of the Bible, which gives a much stronger picture of the state of man by nature, than our Confession. Paul in the first and third chapters of his epistle to the Romans, states it at length, in as strong language as can be used; and in hundreds of other places, we find mankind spoken of as being "in the gall of bitterness and bonds of iniquity." Gen. vi. 5—"God saw that the wickedness of man was great on the earth, and that every imagination of the thoughts of his heart was only evil continually." Gen. viii. 21—"The imagination of man's heart is evil from his youth." But I need not multiply proofs of a fact which, as you say, is proved by every day's observation.

The simple fact of the universal wickedness of mankind, has always proved a great difficulty with those who deny the doctrine of innate depravity. Some have attempted to account for it, from the influence of example—that men are wicked, because they are surrounded with a bad influence. But whence the universal bad example? This is endeavouring to account for a fact, by referring to the fact itself; and is about as wise as to say that men are wicked because they are wicked.

Others have said that it is an abuse of their freedom of will. But why the universal abuse of free will? It is admitted on all hands, that the will is free. But why does it uniformly choose evil? There must be some cause that operates in inclining the will to act as it does. This method of accounting for the fact, is, if possible, more absurd than the other, and is about as consistent with common sense, as to account for the changes of the wind, by the turnings of a weathercock.

Con.—I do not see how we can avoid the conclusion that there is in man an innate propensity inclining him to evil.

Min.—The next step, then, is to inquire whence, and upon what principles came this propensity to evil. If this world be inhabited by a depraved intelligence, how came it to be so? Man was not so created. The evil cannot be imputed to God. The fault must be in man himself. "God made man upright, but they have sought out many inventions," is what the Bible tells us on this point, and to this statement we must all assent. It is admitted, too, on all hands, I believe, that some how, in consequence of the fall of our first parents, all the evil found in the world has been entailed upon their posterity; but the principles upon which this is to be accounted for, is a point much controverted, and about which you say your mind labours.

Some say that there was not any legal connection between Adam and his posterity, and that they had no concern whatever with his sin, but that the present state of mankind is to be accounted for on the simple principle of transmission. As a tree propagates its kind, so the posterity of Adam naturally inherit his nature. The advocates of this doctrine express great abhorrence at the idea of being held in any way legally responsible for the sin of Adam; and represent it as highly tyrannical in God, to hold us responsible for a sin committed so long before we were born. But they forget that they are quarreling with an admitted fact in the government of God. They admit that all evil is entailed upon us, in consequence of Adam's sin, and yet deny that we had any concern with it whatever. Now what could be more tyrannical than this? In the government and providence of God, we are visited with all the tremendous consequences and dreadful evils of a sin, with which we had no concern whatever. If we had no concern with his sin, it is certainly the highest injustice and tyranny to visit us with any of its consequences. How much more consistent with the character of God, and with common sense, to admit the simple fact as it is expressed in our catechism, that we "sinned in him, and fell with him."

Con.—But how could we sin in him.

Min.—Upon the simple principle of representation, which enters into all God's dealings with us. It is easy to understand how a man acts through a representative, or agent. And who would ever think of calling it injustice or tyranny, to hold a person responsible for the actions of his agent, or representative? The people of a State act in and through their representatives in the Legislature. If they make wholesome laws, the people, with themselves, reap the benefit; and if they make unjust and oppressive laws, the people, equally with themselves, are involved in the evil consequences; and in this way the people become liable to all the evils resulting from such mal-administration. It is in this way, upon the principle of representation, that we all "sinned in Adam, and fell with him," and became liable to all the consequences of his sin, equally with himself. This is the sense in which the term "guilt" is used in our Confession. We are not guilty of Adam's sin personally, but liable to punishment on account of it; and it is in this way that we say his sin is imputed to us; that is it is set to our account.

Con.—But is not this doctrine liable to objection, on the ground that we had nothing to do with his appointment as our representative?

Min.– Under the circumstances, it was

impossible that we could select our own agent to act for us; but the simple question to be determined is, was it just, wise, and merciful in God, thus to deal with us on the principle of representation? and when we could not choose our own representative, to choose one for us? Will any one say that it would have been better for the human family that each should have stood singly for himself in the great trial of obedience? In that case we must leave out of view the covenant of grace and the Saviour; for each individual, standing for himself upon the great trial for life or death, can have no reference to another. Then all mankind, from infancy to age—every moment—is on trial; and the moment any one fails in thought, word, or action, then eternal death is the penalty, without a single gleam of hope. The feeble infant, with no distinct conceptions of law or penalty, with almost no power to distinguish between good and evil, unable properly to appreciate the tendencies of conduct, and more than all, without any knowledge that it is placed on such a trial; yet is every moment standing in such a relation to God and his law, that the indulgence of a single sinful feeling brings upon it all the weight of the infinite penalty of God's law. Now, does it not display the goodness of God to put that infant on trial, in the person of such a perfect being as Adam? And when the Bible reveals the fact, that this was actually done, who, in the name of common sense, and of wisdom and goodness, can find fault, and say it was unjust and tyrannical?

But, to put the matter in a still more favourable light, suppose that all should be kept by God until maturity, and then put on trial; and even allowing them to be as fully endowed with moral strength as Adam was, yet placed upon the awfully solemn trial, under such circumstances, that the moment any one should sin, in thought, word, or deed, his case is for ever as hopeless as that of the fallen angels, (who stood precisely in those circumstances,) and the case is very little better. Now, is there any one, of all Adam's race, who would prefer thus to be placed? Does it not show in a striking light the wisdom and goodness of God, in thus putting us on trial in our original progenitor, and thereby increasing, more than ten thousand-fold, his motives to obedience? Does not the principle of representation, upon which God deals with us, commend itself to the plainest dictates of reason and common sense? And who will find fault with his Maker for selecting a representative for us, when we could not, under the circumstances, choose one ourselves? And moreover, he appointed the very person, whom all mankind would have chosen, if it could have been left to them.

Con.—Is this what is meant in the Catechism by the "covenant," which it says was "made with Adam, not only for himself, but for his posterity?"

Min.—Yes; the agreement entered into between God and Adam, whereby he stood as our representative, is called a covenant, because there were certain stipulations to be fulfilled, and a reward promised; and on the other hand, a penalty threatened for the breach of it.

Con.—But is all this clearly revealed in the Bible?

Min.—We are not told, in express words, that there was a covenant made between God and Adam; and the opposers of the doctrine have attempted to triumph, because it is not stated in so many words that there was such a covenant transaction. But such attempts at triumph are, to say the least, very silly. I once heard a Socinian triumph in the same way, because he said the words "divinity of Christ," were not to be found in the Bible. And a Universalist, also, once in my hearing, pretended to triumph, because he said the words "future punishment," were not found in the Bible. You can easily perceive that such things only betray their weakness. The question is not, Are the exact words, by which we express an idea, found in the Bible; but is the idea there plainly taught? The idea of the representative character of Adam, and of his covenant relation to us, is as plainly taught in the Bible as almost any other truth. Rom. v. 19—"By one man's disobedience many were made sinners." Verse 12—"By one man sin entered into the world, and death by sin, and so death passed upon all men, for that all have sinned." We are here taught as plainly as can be, that death is the consequence of sin; and the reason that all die, is, "that all have sinned." Now, we know that many die in infancy, before any actual sin can be laid to their charge. Then how have they sinned? It is impossible to explain it on any other supposition, than that they sinned in Adam; and they could not sin in him in any other way, but by representation.

Con—Do you then believe that those dying in infancy will be condemned on account of their original sin?

Min.—That is not a necessary conclusion. Reasoning from analogy, we may conclude that it is consistent with God's character and manner of dealing with mankind, to save them through the atonement of Christ. Paul tells us, Rom. v. 14—that "death reigned from Adam to Moses, even over them that had not sinned, after the similitude of Adam's transgression"—that is, infants who had not sinned actually. Now, seeing that they are involved in the consequences of Adam's sin, without actual participation, they may be included in the purpose of mercy through Christ, without actual participation by faith. But if saved they will be saved as redeemed sinners, and will unite with all the host of God's elect, in singing "glory to the Lamb that redeemed us, and washed us in his blood." Now, it is plain that they cannot be redeemed, if they are not lost; they cannot be washed, if they are not polluted; they cannot be saved through Christ, if they are not sinners. If they are saved through Christ, it is an incontrovertible proof that they are sinners through Adam.

But further, Paul says, Rom. v. 18—"By the offence of one, judgment came upon all men to condemnation." If this does not prove that all men are liable to condemnation on account of the sin of Adam, language has no meaning. And there is no way that they could become thus liable, but by sustaining to him a covenant relation, such as I have spoken of. Many other passages are equally clear in teaching the same truth, by plain and necessary deduction, which I need not enumerate. But we are not left to this mode of proof entirely. It is plainly manifest, that every item essential to a covenant, is contained in the transaction between God and Adam; and the term "covenant," is given to it by Hosea, vii. 9—"They like men have transgressed the covenant." The literal rendering of the Hebrew is, "They like Adam have transgressed the covenant." The Hebrew phrase, "*ke Adam*," which is here used, is so rendered in Job xxxi. 33—"If I covered my transgression, as Adam," &c.; from which it is plain that the idea of a covenant with Adam was familiar to the inspired writers.

I have now given a few, and only a few, of the many arguments that might be drawn from reason and the Bible, as well as from facts, to prove the representative character of Adam, and our covenant relation to him, on the ground of which his sin is imputed to his posterity; and they consequently inherit a sinful nature, having "sinned in him, and fallen with him in his first transgression." Enough, however, has been said, I think, to show you that the doctrine of our Confession of Faith on this subject, is the doctrine of the Bible, and of common sense.

Con.—My mind is entirely relieved of its difficulty; and I find the doctrine of imputation, so far as it respects Adam's sin, is far different from what I had conceived it to be.

Min.—The other part of the doctrine, viz: the imputation of Christ's righteousness as our only dependence for salvation, I presume you understand more clearly.

Con.—I have made it my only dependence, and rejoice to do so; but still I would be glad to understand it more fully, as my Methodist neighbour tells me that faith, and good works are, at least in part, the meritorious ground of my justification.

Min.--We will take up that subject in our nex; conversation.

DIALOGUE VIII.

FREE GRACE.

Minister.—In establishing the doctrine of the imputed righteousness of Christ, as the only ground of our justification in the sight of God, it is important, in the first place, to have a clear understanding of our relations to him, and the claims of his law.

Convert.—Are we still under obligations to obey the law of God, notwithstanding we have broken it and incurred its penalty?

Min.—The fact that we have broken God's law, cannot free us from obligations to serve and obey him, in the smallest degree. But we are speaking now, more particularly, of what is necessary to escape the penalty justly due us as sinners. It is said by some that God has relaxed the original terms upon which eternal life was first promised, and that he has been graciously pleased, for Christ's sake, to make a new covenant with man, in which he promises to pardon our sins if we repent; and since we cannot render perfect obedience during all our life, he will accept of our imperfect obedience, if it be sincere. This, I suppose, is the opinion of your Methodist neighbour, whom you mentioned as maintaining, that we are justified, in part at least, by works. But this is only an attempt to "establish our own righteousness," and is not only unscriptural, but absurd. The law of God is a transcript of his character, and was so intended to be. "Be ye holy, for I am holy," was the sanction that accompanied it; and who will dare to set up a lower standard? If its claims are let down, then it is abrogated, and a new one set up through Christ. But Christ says expressly, that he "came not to destroy, but to fulfill." Besides, if there be a change in God's law, it is no longer to us a transcript of his character, and cannot be a perfect standard of holiness. Consequently, too, the principles of his government are changed; and things which were once sins, cannot now be so accounted; and things that were once duties, are now dispensed with, which casts a severe, if not impious, reflection upon both the Governor and his law. It is, in fact, nothing more than salvation by works, and casts away altogether the necessity of a Saviour; for if the high authority of the law may give way for the accommodation of a criminal, why was it necessary that any obedience or satisfaction should be rendered to it by another in his stead? The obedience and sufferings of the Saviour were, in that case, mere works of supererogation, given to a law, which, after all, did not necessarily demand them.

Con.—But may we not suppose that the sufferings of Christ were intended to show God's hatred of sin in such a light, that he might consistently pardon sin, without an impeachment of his law or character, when the sinner sincerely repents?

Min.—The sufferings of the Saviour do exhibit, in a very striking light, the great evil of sin; and it was no doubt intended that they should do so. But if we stop there, we make the atonement a very small matter. It represents God as making a show of respect for his law and government, which, in fact, does not exist, if he can look over a violation of it without the satisfaction it demands; and the atonement of the Son of God was nothing more than this governmental display, which would be unworthy of an earthly king. This theory is, however, becoming very popular at the present day; and what is more strange, it is advocated by some who call themselves Presbyterians, and profess attachment to the Confession of Faith, though they are not now in our connection. But to see in a still clearer light the unreasonableness of these systems, we have only to consider what are in reality the claims of God's law, as laid down in the Bible, which, I have already said, is necessary to a right understanding of the subject. "Love the Lord with all thy heart, and with all thy soul, and with all thy strength, and with all thy mind, and thy neighbour as thyself," is what God claims of all his intelligent creatures. And will any one say he asks too much, or that it would be consistent with his character to accept of anything less? "God is love;" and in this summary of his law he has given us a transcript of his character. It is the same grand principle that binds angels, and all the intelligent universe. It is like himself, and all his works; simple, yet grand, majestic, and glorious in its simplicity. It extends to every faculty and power of the creature, "heart, soul, strength, and mind;" and, being thus the basis, or grand principle of his moral government, it is as unchangeable as himself. The moment he should dispense with any of its requirements, and accept from a creature an obedience that was defective, the stabilities of his throne would be undermined. Hence, Christ says, that "till heaven and earth pass, one jot or one tittle shall in no wise pass from the law, till all be fulfilled. Think not that I am come to destroy the law, or the prophets. I am not come to destroy, but to fulfill."—Matt. v. 17, 18. It is, therefore, not only absurd, but impious, to plead that the law is changed, for the accommodation of sinful man. Sooner may we expect Jehovah to annihilate universal creation, than give up "one jot or one tittle" of that law, which is the transcript of his character. Now, it is this law, which claims obedience originally from us, and its claims we must answer in ourselves, or by another, if we would inherit eternal life; and I presume I need not stay to prove, that no sinner of Adam's race can, in himself, answer its demands.

It is proper, also, that we should notice here the penalty by which obedience to the law of God is enforced. It corresponds with the law in its greatness and justice. Death, with all the dreadful consequences which the Bible attaches to that term, when speaking of it as a penalty threatened, is a punishment in which will be exhibited for ever the greatness, justice, and majesty of God, and his law.

We, therefore, as sinners, having incurred this penalty, the law has a two-fold claim upon us—satisfaction and restitution. The law must be satisfied, to place us on terms of reconciliation with God; and then it requires complete and perfect obedience to entitle us to life. It is equally plain, that no finite creature can give to the law the infinite satisfaction it requires; and this is one reason that the punishment of the wicked must be eternal.

Con.—Mankind are then, by nature, in a very wretched condition.

Min.—That is very true; and this is no doubt one reason that so much opposition is manifested toward the doctrines of grace. Volumes have been written, the Scriptures have been perverted, and every expedient has been tried, to prove that the spiritual condition of mankind is not so bad. But the only effect that can result from it, is to make sinners more careless. It is always best for us to know the worst of our spiritual condition. If there were no remedy provided, it would be humane to endeavour, as far as possible, to allay fears that could be of no avail. But when God has graciously provided a remedy, it is unfaithfulness to the Saviour, and cruelty to the souls of men, to attempt to hide, in the smallest degree, their real condition.

But this brings us to speak of what God, in infinite mercy, has done to save us from this wretched condition. The Son of God took upon himself to answer the claims of the law in our stead, both as it respects obedience and satisfaction, and in both respects satisfied its claims to the full. By his obedience and sufferings he has wrought out a righteousness, on the ground of which we may be accepted. And here again, God deals with us on the principle of representation. The Saviour stood, and still stands, as our representative and agent. Our sins were imputed to him—that is, they were set to his account—he engaged to answer for them, and was thus treated as a sinner. On the other hand, his righteousness is imputed to us; that is, it is set to our account, and we are treated as righteous, on the ground of what he has done for us. All this is briefly, yet clearly expressed in our Confession of Faith and Catechisms. "Justification is an act of God's free grace, wherein he pardoneth all our sins, and accepteth us as righteous in his sight, only for the righteousness of Christ imputed to us, and received by faith alone."—Shorter Cat., Quest. 33.

Con.—What do you understand by *faith*, as you use the term in this connection?

Min.—It is simply the act of the soul in casting itself upon Christ, and trusting to his righteousness for salvation; or, as our catechism expresses it, "Faith in Jesus Christ is a saving grace, whereby we receive and rest upon him alone for salvation, as he is offered to us in the Gospel."—Quest. 86. Christ is offered us in the Gospel, as a Saviour who has fulfilled the law, and satisfied the justice of God in our stead; and we are invited to come, and be saved through him. When we accept of him as our Saviour, and cast ourselves upon him for salvation, the act of the soul in so doing is faith; and hence, in this sense, it is called "saving faith." It is then that the righteousness of Christ is set to our account, and made ours through faith.

Con.—Is faith, then, a necessary condition of our salvation?

Min.—It is necessary, but can hardly be called a condition, in the sense in which the term is generally used; at least it is not a meritorious condition. There can be no merit in simply accepting a thing offered, though it is necessary that we accept it before it can be ours. It is in this sense that faith is necessary to our salva tion. We must accept of the salvation offered through Christ; and in the acceptance of it, God makes it over to us. Hence, the catechism says, it is "received by faith alone." And from this, also, you will be able to understand the numerous texts of Scripture which speak of salvation by faith. "He that believeth and is baptized shall be saved, but he that believeth not shall be damned."—Mark xvi. 16. "Believe on the Lord Jesus Christ, and thou shalt be saved."—Acts xvi. 31, &c. We are also said to be "justified by faith."—Rom. v. 1. "Therefore it is of faith, that it might be by grace."—Rom. iv. 16. "Justified freely by his grace through the redemption that is in Christ Jesus."—Rom. iii. 24. Besides many other passages, which I need not enumerate.

Con.—But a difficulty presents itself to my mind here, respecting the atonement of Christ, and which I have heard urged against the doctrine of an infinite satisfaction being given, or the full penalty of the law endured by him. How could he give an infinite satisfaction in so short a period? He did not suffer eternally, nor did he suffer remorse, &c., which was due the sinner.

Min.—Eternal death, strictly speaking, was not the penalty of the law. It became so from the nature of the persons incurring it. They are finite, and cannot give the full satisfaction, in all conceivable time; therefore, they must atone for their sins eternally. But an infinite being may give infinite value to an atonement in time. Thus, the divinity of the Son of God stamps his atonement with infinity. We are told he "magnified the law, and made it honourable." No finite being could thus magnify the law, or show its greatness and dignity in any clearer light, because it was made for them, and all owe it obedience. But the Son of God, being infinite in all the perfections of Deity, did not owe it obedience for himself; and when he made it the rule of his life, and condescended to satisfy its claims, he "magnified it, and made it honourable," in a light in which it never was before. Its holiness, justice, majesty, and excellence, are displayed in a more glorious light than they could have been in any other conceivable way. The law is more honoured and magnified by the obedience and satisfaction rendered to it by the Son of God, than it could have been by the perfect obedience and eternal death of all the intelligent creatures in the universe. Hence, the apostle calls it "the righteousness of God."—Rom. iii. 21, 22, and in several other places. It is this obedience and satisfaction of the Son of God, that constituted the glorious righteousness, on the ground of which God has offered salvation to all who believe on his Son. It is a righteousness as great, perfect, holy, infinite, and glorious as God himself; a righteousness, on the ground of which he can be just, and yet the justifier of every one who will believe, however sinful and polluted he may be. Nay, more: it is a righteousness, on the ground of which he cannot only be barely just, but also glorious in its exercise. His justice, holiness, truth, mercy, and every attribute, will be for ever glorified in the justification extended to every believing sinner, through the glorious righteousness of his Son.

Now, when God has lavished his love and wisdom on such a plan of salvation, so glorifying to himself, and so suitable for us, how strange that men, in the pride of opinion, will endeavour to find out another! And when we are offered such a righteousness as the ground of our salvation, we may well ask whether any one truly loves the Saviour, who will bring up his own faith and obedience, and plead them before God as meriting salvation; as if the glorious righteousness of the Son of God were not sufficient.

Con.—It cannot be salvation by grace, if we merit it in any degree ourselves. Any true Christian will desire to ascribe all the glory to his Saviour. At least it so seems to me. It surely contributes in no small degree to the enjoyment of the believing sinner, to ascribe all the praise to his Saviour.

Min.—Let us now see what the Bible says on these points. And first let us examine what proofs it contains that our sins were imputed to Christ, and that he took our place under the law. Isa. liii. 4, 5—"Surely he hath borne our griefs and carried our sorrows. * * But he was wounded for our transgressions; he was bruised for our iniquities; the chastisement of our peace was upon him; and with his stripes we are healed. All we like sheep have gone astray; we have turned every one to his own way; and the Lord hath laid on him the iniquity of us all." Verse 11—"By his knowledge shall my righteous servant justify many, for he shall bear their iniquities." Verse 12—"He bare the sin of many." 2 Cor. v. 21—"He hath made him to be sin for us, * * that we might be made the righteousness of God in him." Here both truths are plainly stated, that our sins are set to his account, and his righteousness to ours.

There is no other conceivable sense in which he could be "made sin," or we "made the righteousness of God." 1 Pet. ii. 24—"His own self bare our sins in his own body on the tree; by whose stripes ye are healed." Here, again, both truths are thrown together. 1 Pet. iii. 18—"Christ also hath once suffered for sin, the just for the unjust, that he might bring us to God." These, with all the texts which speak of him as "dying for us," and being a "propitiation for us," and a "propitiation for our sins," (of which kind hundreds might be adduced,) prove the doctrine of his substitution in our stead, as plainly as language can prove it. If they do not prove that the death of Christ was a true and proper sacrifice for sin in our stead, human language cannot state it.

That his righteousness is imputed to us, is taught in language equally plain. And I would observe that all the passages which deny salvation by "works," the "deeds of the law," &c., by necessary implication, prove that we are saved only by the righteousness of Christ. Rom. iii. 20—28—"Therefore by the deeds of the law shall no flesh be justified in his sight. But now the righteousness of God without the law is manifested, * * even the righteousness of God, which is by faith of Jesus Christ, unto all, and upon all them that believe. Being justified freely by his grace through the redemption that is in Christ Jesus, whom God hath set forth to be a propitiation through faith in his blood, to declare his righteousness for the remission of sins that are past, through the forbearance of God. To declare, I say, at this time, his righteousness that he might be just and the justifier of him which believeth on Jesus. Where is boasting then? It is excluded. By what law? Of works? Nay; but by the law of faith. Therefore, we conclude that a man is justified by faith, without the deeds of the law." Now, is it not strange that any one pretending to common sense, and to be guided by the Bible, would, in the face of all this plain and unequivocal language, uphold salvation by works, in any degree whatever? But further still, the apostle reasons the case at length in the fourth chapter; and in the fifth, in drawing a parallel between Christ and Adam, states the doctrine again with equal plainness. Rom. v. 18—"By the righteousness of one, the free gift came upon all men unto justification of life." Verse 19—"By the obedience of one shall many be made righteous." Chap. x. 3, 4—"But they being ignorant of God's righteousness, and going about to establish their own righteousness, have not submitted themselves to the righteousness of God. For Christ is the end of the law for righteousness to every one that believeth." Phil. iii. 9—"That I may win Christ and be found in him, not having mine own righteousness, which is of the law, but that which is through the faith of Christ, the righteousness which is of God by faith." But I need not multiply quotations, which might be done to almost any extent.

Con.—I find that the Calvinistic doctrines are justly styled the doctrines of grace, and yet those who deny them, lay strong claims to a system of "free grace," and "free salvation."

Min.—It is only another of their inconsistencies. How can that be free, which is merited or bought by works? If our good works merit salvation, it is a contradiction in terms to call it free. So Paul reasons, Rom. iv. 4—"To him that worketh is the reward not reckoned of grace, but of debt." And further, verse 16—"Therefore it is of faith, that it might be by grace." And again, Rom. xi. 6—"If it be of works, then it is no more grace." So, according to Paul, they can lay no claim to the doctrine of a "free salvation," who maintain that it is in any sense by works.

DIALOGUE IX.

GOOD WORKS.

Convert.—Since our last conversation I have been reflecting upon the doctrine of imputation, and examining the Bible, and find that it is one of its plainest doctrines. And in taking all its features, and viewing them together, they present a very grand scheme, and show the glorious work of redemption in a light that I think must surely recommend it to any burdened and heart-broken sinner, seeking to escape the wrath of God. And though I feel that it is the only doctrine upon which I can safely depend, yet is it not liable to objection, on the ground that it leaves good works and holy living entirely out of view?

Minister.—It only leaves them out of view as the meritorious ground of our salvation; but in every other respect it secures and establishes them. This is the very objection which Paul meets in the last verse of the third chapter of his epistle to the Romans. He lays down, in language that cannot well be misunderstood, the truth that we are "justified by faith, without the deeds of the law;" and then, knowing that the objection you speak of would be urged against it, he anticipates it in the last verse: "Do we then make void the law through faith?" That is, if we by faith place all our dependence for salvation upon the righteousness of Christ, and none upon our own obedience to the law, will it not make us careless about that obedience, and lead us to think that the law has no further claims upon us, and thus "make void the law," as requiring of us a holy life? But how does he answer it? "God forbid: yea, we establish the law." This might be sufficient; but it will not be amiss to look a little further, and see how faith establishes the law. We have already seen how it establishes the law, in answering all its claims through the righteousness of Christ; and that it establishes it also as the believer's rule of life, is equally plain. To show this, I need not go further than your own experience. When you first obtained a hope of salvation through Christ, what seemed to be the most prominent feeling of your heart?

Con.—I was overwhelmed with a sense of the love of God, as manifested through the Saviour. And when I thought of the Son of God, suffering and dying to redeem me from hell, I felt as if it would be the joy of my life to serve him with my whole heart.

Min.—Do you think it possible for any one to exercise faith in Christ for salvation, without experiencing, in some degree, the same feelings of love and devotion?

Con.—I do not see how it is possible for any one to look to the Son of God as his Saviour, without loving and desiring to serve him; and at the same time, desiring to be made holy, and conformed to his image and example.

Min.—You have now answered the objection in your own experience, which is, in a greater or less degree, the experience of every true Christian. True faith will never be found in the heart of any one, without producing its legitimate effects, love to Christ, hatred of sin, and a desire after holiness, and conformity to the law of God in all its parts. So Paul describes it. Gal. v. 6—"Faith which worketh by love." And Peter, in Acts xv. 9, ascribes to it the effect of "purifying the heart." And in Acts xxvi. 18, we are said to be "sanctified by faith." So it is plain, both from Christian experience and from Scripture, that the effect of faith is to produce love and holiness in the heart of the believer; and thus his sanctification is carried on. Faith is the first act of a regenerated soul; and then immediately the work of sanctification commences, which is carried on through the instrumentality of faith. It sanctifies as well as justifies. Just as surely as any one has the faith that justifies, he has also the faith that sanctifies. It is impossible to separate them. It is true, faith is not meritorious in either case, but only instrumental; but it is always just as surely instrumental of the one as of the other. It is absurd to suppose that any one can have faith in Christ, that is, depend upon him for salvation, without loving him; and it is equally absurd to suppose that any one could love him, without at the same time desiring to obey all his commands. And I know not how any true Christian, who really loves his Saviour, and understands his own heart, can plead the objection that an entire dependence upon Christ for salvation, weakens his sense of obligation and "makes void the law." It is a reflection cast upon true religion, unworthy of a Christian.

All this is plainly taught in our Confession of Faith, as well as the Bible. Chap. 11, sec. 2--"Faith, thus receiving and resting on Christ and his righteousness, is the alone instrument of justification; yet it is not alone, in the person justified, but is ever accompanied with all other saving graces; and is no dead faith, but worketh by love." Again, chap. 16, sec. 2—"These good works, done in obedience to God's commandments, are the fruits and evidences of a true and lively faith," &c. And that faith should, and does produce these effects, is surely a dictate of common sense. Let any one have true faith, and then holiness of heart and life is a certain consequence.

Con.—But is faith not sometimes to be understood in a more extended sense, than simply depending on and trusting in Christ for salvation?

Min.—Though this is its principal act, it extends to, and acts upon, everything that God has revealed. As it is expressed in our Confession, chap. 14, sec. 2—"By this faith a Christian believeth to be true whatsoever is revealed in the word, for the authority of God himself speaking therein; and acteth differently upon that which each particular passage thereof containeth; yielding obedience to the commands, trembling at the threatenings, and embracing the promises of God for this life, and that which is to come," &c. The apostle also says, "By faith we know the worlds were made," &c. And again, "He that cometh to God must believe that he is, and that he is the rewarder of them that diligently seek him." But faith in all these acts is subordinate, and dependent for its right exercise upon the principal act. It is only when we are brought to look to God through Christ, that we have right views of his character as he is revealed in his word, and admit with the heart all his claims. Then we see, in a true light, what he says of the evil of sin, the justness of our condemnation, and the freeness of his mercy and grace in our justification. Then, when we look into his word, all its blessed truths come home to our hearts, with a point and clearness before unknown. Its threatenings and promises, precepts and exhortations, have a peculiar force and pungency, which tell upon our conduct and pursuits, and produce earnest desires for sincere and constant obedience. "With the heart, man believeth unto righteousness." Thus faith secures holiness; and view it as we may, either in its principal act of dependence on Christ for salvation, or in its cordial acceptance and approval of all the other truths of God's word, it "establishes the law" as the great rule of obedience, in conformity to which the believer strives to live. "Working by love," which is "the fulfilling of the law," it secures this glorious result, wherever it is found in sincerity and truth.

Thus, the plan of salvation exhibits the wisdom of God in all its features. It saves lost sinners, transforms them from sin, and secures the practice of holiness, yet in a way that excludes boasting or self-glorification in the smallest degree, and gives all the praise to God.

Con.—But is there not some sense in which faith and holiness commend us to God?

Min.—They commend us to God as obedient children striving after conformity to his law, and reflecting his image. Eph. v. 1, 2—"Be ye followers of God as dear children, and walk in love, as Christ also hath loved us, and given himself for us." Of such Paul says, Rom. ii. 29—"Whose praise is not of men, but of God." Indeed, the Scriptures everywhere teach that good works, by which I mean all the graces of piety brought out into active operation, are pleasing to God; and only in their performance can we expect his blessing, and the approving smiles of his countenance. And this is said to be one grand object of salvation. Tit. ii. 14—"That he might purify to himself a peculiar people, zealous of good works." Besides, they are evidences of the sincerity of our faith, both to God and man. It is only in their performance that we can "let our light shine," and exhibit to the world the excellency of that religion we profess. They are the true tests of Christian love; and even in the sight of God prove our faith to be of the right kind. As he said to Abraham, "Now I know that thou fearest God." And the apostle James tells us, that "by works his faith was made perfect."—James ii. 22. That is, it was proved to be of the right kind.

Con.—But does not James say in the same connection, that Abraham was justified by works? And how is this to be reconciled with the language of Paul?

Min.—The most common interpretation given to the language of James is, that he was speaking of our justification in the sight of men. And it is true, that it is only by good works that we can sustain a Christian character. But the apostle evidently speaks of justification in the sight of God; for he says in the 14th verse, "Can faith save him?" The doctrines called Antinomianism were prevalent in the days of the apostle, which taught that the gospel released believers from obedience to the law, and it is very evident that it was against this that James was writing, and also no doubt to refute the doctrine that justifying faith was a mere speculative belief, which produced no sanctifying influence upon the heart. In verse 14 he says, "What doth it profit, my brethren, though a man say he have faith and have not works? can faith save him?" That is, can that kind of faith save him? In the original it is "*he pistis*," the faith, or the kind of faith mentioned. In the 19th verse he says, "Thou believest there is one God; thou dost well; the devils also believe and tremble." From this it is very plain that the faith of which he is speaking, and which he says cannot save a man, is the same that the devils have; and he adds in the following verses, "Wilt thou know, O vain man, that faith without works is dead? Was not Abraham, our father, justified by works when he had offered Isaac his son upon the altar? Seest thou how faith wrought with his works, and by works was faith made perfect? And the Scripture was fulfilled which saith, Abraham believed God, and it was imputed unto him for righteousness. Ye see, then, how that by works a man is justified, and not by faith only." The Scripture, which the apostle says was fulfilled by Abraham offering his son, is Gen. xv. 6. "And he believed in the Lord, and he counted it to him for righteousness." The faith that Abraham exercised in this instance was belief and confidence in the promise that he should have a son, including the promise of a Savior. It was by this act of faith that Abraham was justified, as Paul tells us in Rom. iv. 3, 10, 11—"Abraham believed God, and it was counted unto him for righteousness." "How was it then reckoned? When he was in circumcision, or in uncircumcision? Not in circumcision, but in uncircumcision. And he received the sign of circumcision, a seal of the righteousness of the faith which he had, yet being uncircumcised."

Here both apostles are plainly together, in teaching that Abraham was justified by that act of faith. But this was more than twenty years before the offering of his son, in which James says this Scripture was fulfilled. Now, will any one pretend that the apostle intended to teach, that Abraham was not justified until he offered his son? This would be inconsistent both with scripture and common sense, and the language of the apostle himself. In what sense, then, was this scripture fulfilled in the offering of his son? Plainly in this, that he thereby proved his faith to be of the right kind, a genuine faith of the gospel, working by love, and producing obedience to the commands of God. There is no other conceivable sense in which it could be fulfilled. Neither can we suppose that the apostle intended to teach, that true evangelical faith is ever found without good works; and unless we deny a plain passage of scripture, written by Moses, and quoted by both James and Paul, we must conclude that he only intended to teach, that we cannot be justified by a "dead faith," which is "without works;" and that a believing, active faith, which "works by love and purifies the heart," is necessary to our justification. For he expressly says, that "Abraham's faith was perfected by his works," that is, he showed thereby that it was not a dead faith. Therefore we are "justified by works, and not by faith only," inasmuch as they are the evidence and certain fruits of a justifying faith. A faith that does not produce them is not only useless, but is worse than useless. It is a cheat, an injury to ourselves and others. When we, in the exercise of faith, confide ourselves to Christ for salvation, we do it upon his own terms, one of which is, to do whatsoever he commands. To do this is not only the obligation, but the desire of every one who is truly united to him by faith. He who has the good works which spring from true faith is justified, but he who has them not is not justified, for they are inseparable. "Without holiness no man shall see the Lord."

Con.—But is there not some sense in which our good works merit reward?

Min.—They will be rewarded; but it will still be of grace. Christ tells us, Luke xvii. 10—"When ye shall have done all these things which are commanded you, say, we are unprofitable servants; we have done that which was our duty to do." Still they will all be graciously rewarded. Matt. x. 42—"A cup of cold water given to a disciple in the name of a disciple, shall not lose its reward." Moses, we are told, Heb. xi. 26, "had respect unto the recompense of reward." We need not fear that God will overlook anything done with love to him through faith in his Son. It is revealed as one great ingredient in our happiness in heaven, that "our works shall follow us."—Rev. xiv. 13. We need not fear to expect too much at the hand of God. Only let us expect it in the right way, "not of debt, but of grace." Our works follow us in heaven. They do not go before, to open the heavenly gates, or gain us access there. That is done by our Saviour. But they follow us, and shall be taken account of by our Saviour. "I was an hungered, and ye gave me meat," &c. And whilst we shall rejoice in the gracious and glorious reward which he condescends to bestow upon our poor service, the burden of our song shall be "to the praise of the glory of his grace."—Eph. i. 6.

Con.—There is a passage of Scripture that I have met with somewhere, which says, "whatsoever is not of faith, is sin;" which I found difficult to understand; but I think I now begin to see its meaning. As faith is the foundation of the other graces, nothing is acceptable to God which does not flow from right feelings. But still, is there nothing good in the outward morality and upright conduct of those who are out of Christ?

Min.—This involves the doctrine of ability, or what a man can do, and what he cannot do, in his natural state, which we wil consider at our next interview.

DIALOGUE X.

INABILITY.

Convert.—In examining the Confession of Faith, since our last interview, I find, in chapter 9, sec. 3, the following language, respecting man's inability; "Man, by his fall into a state of sin, hath wholly lost all ability of will to any spiritual good, accompanying salvation; so, as a natural man, being altogether averse from that which is good, and dead in sin, is not able, by his own strength, to convert himself, or prepare himself thereunto."

But the Bible commands men to repent and believe, and to make to themselves new hearts, &c. Now, is there not a seeming inconsistency in commanding what there is no ability to perform?

Minister.—There can be no inconsistency in commanding any one to the extent of his obligation. Whatever is the duty of any one, God has a right to command, regardless of inability, when that inability is brought on by the sinner himself, and is in itself wrong. It is surely the duty of all to love God It is a plain dictate of common sense, that when any one has done wrong, he ought to repent of it. But how can he repent of it if he loves the wrong? We know that all men naturally love sin, and hate God. How can they repent of sin while they love it? or how can they love God while they hate him? This is the "inability of will," of which the Confession speaks. The will is influenced in choosing and refusing, by the state of the heart. It is this that always gives weight to the motives presented. Whilst the heart is filled with enmity to God, all motives to love him are presented in vain. Now, the simple question is, can a man change his own heart? What resources has he within himself, that he can bring to bear upon the deep rooted enmity of his heart, that will produce such a change in the inner man, as to fill him with love for that which he hates? The only faculty that could possibly have any such effect, is the understanding, or judgment; but it is so darkened, that it can have no proper conception of holy and spiritual things. "The natural man," says Paul, 1 Cor. ii. 14, "receiveth not the things of the Spirit of God, for they are foolishness unto him; neither can he know them, because they are spiritually discerned." The apostle is contrasting the "spiritual" and "natural man," that is, the regenerate and unregenerate, and this is what he tells us of the unregenerate. And the language he uses is much stronger than that used in our confession. "The natural man receiveth not the things of the Spirit of God." He rejects them. All the motives by which their acceptance may be urged, are entirely without avail. And why? Because "they are foolishness unto him"—he has no proper conception of them. "Neither can he know them." He can have no proper understanding of their value, excellence, or necessity, "because they are spiritually discerned." In order to see them aright, and appreciate them, he must be made a "spiritual man." His understanding must be enlightened, and his affections changed. How any one can take a plain common sense view of this passage of Scripture alone, in its obvious sense, and yet contend for the doctrine of full ability, I am at a loss to see. Yet, it is equally plain, that those very things to which the "natural man" is thus wholly disinclined, he is under the strongest obligation to perform. It is his duty to love God with all his heart, and to "receive the things of the Spirit of God," and practise upon them—to repent of his sins, and to turn to God. Hence, it is perfectly consistent for God to command the sinner thus to do. It would be giving up the claims of his law if he did not.

Con.—But is not the inability in the case inconsistent with the obligation?

Min.—The idea that ability is the measure of obligation is not uncommon; and of late has been widely propagated as an axiom in morals and theology, and is hailed by many as a new discovery, that is to clear up the knotty points of perfect freedom of will, and absolute dependence on God. It is boldly asserted, that man is under no obligation to do anything, for which he has not full and perfect ability in himself. But this position is one of the most glaring absurdities to be found in the whole catalogue of errors, now afloat. If inability cancels obligation, Satan is under no obligation to love God, and his fiendish enmity to God and immortal souls is no sin. If I murder the head of a helpless family, I am only accountable for the murder, and not for the wretchedness and misery that I thus bring upon the family, which I have no power to alleviate. My inability to soothe the sorrows, and alleviate the wants of the widow and orphans, cancels my obligation. There is no escape from such dreadful consequences of the doctrine, except its abettors will go one step further back, and say that God is the author of man's inability to obey his commands. This, I presume, none will dare do. Man's inability is his own fault; and to pretend that it frees him from obligation, subverts all moral government. Sin, then, is its own apology. The sinner can stand up boldly and say, I am not able in myself to love God. I hate him so that I cannot love him; therefore I am not under obligation to love him. It lifts the sinner above the law of God. He requires obedience; the sinner disables himself; and, therefore, he is not bound to obey. Rebellion against God is then the only sure road to independence. But I need not follow such absurdities further. You can see clearly, that man's inability to obey the law of God, can in no sense free him from obligation.

Con.—But has not man some kind of ability? I have some where in the course of my reading met with the doctrine that man is naturally able to love and serve God, but morally unable—that is, he could if he would.

Min.—That the sinner's inability is moral, is admitted on all hands; and that it is of such a nature that he could obey if he would, is not, I believe, denied by any. But this is the same as saying he could love God, if he loved him. The unwillingness to obey—the aversion to God, and holiness—is the inability in the case. This is the moral state of the soul; it is wickedly unwilling, and therefore unable, without a gracious change. Until such a change is effected, the sinner never will love God, and in this sense, using the language of the Bible, we say he cannot, that is, there is no cause to produce the effect. Christ says, "No man can come to me, except the Father which has sent me, draw him." And, again, he shows the nature of this inability: "Ye will not come to me, that ye might have life."

If those who contend that the sinner has a natural ability, would tell us plainly what they mean by it, and what it amounts to, we would know better how to answer them. If they mean by it that he has all his natural faculties, we admit it. But if these are not a sufficient cause to produce the effect, why contend that they constitute an ability to do that which they cannot do? Man has ability to love, and therefore has ability to love God, is about the amount of their reasoning. But this is about as wise as to say, that because it is the nature of water to flow, it therefore has a natural ability to flow up hill. This strikes you as an amusing absurdity; but it is not a whit more absurd than to contend, because man has all his natural faculties, that, therefore, he has a natural ability to love God. The nature of water is a cause just as adequate to the production of the effect in the one case, as the nature of man in the other. All his affections and inclinations are turned away from God, and flow in an opposite direction.

Con.—But we daily see men of the world living in some degree according to the commands of God. We see honesty, sobriety, and in short, morality in all its moral beauty, exhibited in the lives of unregenerate men. Does not this contradict the idea of a total inability to do good?

Min.—Man has an ability to do many things that are good in themselves, and indeed, to do anything predicable of his nature as man, which he chooses to do, or in other words, that he is willing to do. As it respects outward morality, many motives may be brought to bear, which will induce men to live in accordance with its rules, viz. a respect for public opinion, a desire of reputation, &c.,—and not unfrequently, a hope that thereby they may recommend themselves to God, and finally escape hell. Sometimes, indeed, it is their enmity to God and religion, that induces them to live lives of strict morality, that thereby they may compare with the Christian, whom they watch with an eagle eye, and endeavour to magnify his failures, in order to bring reproach upon religion. In all these instances, however, it is easy to see that "God is not in all their thoughts." Their hearts are still alienated from him, and they refuse to acknowledge his authority. They live morally, not because God has required it, but from some other selfish motive. They refuse to pray, neglect and violate the Sabbath, refuse to repent and confess the Son of God, neglect or oppose religion, and in short exhibit very plainly the enmity of their hearts to God. It is true, they will not admit that they hate God, and perhaps they think they do not; but if they hate religion and holiness, they hate God, for this is his character. They cannot hate the one without hating the other, or love the one without loving the other. If any one love God, he will love religion, and yield himself in obedience to its dictates; and if he hate religion, he hates God. They are inseparable. Hence, Paul says, Rom. viii. 7—"The carnal mind is enmity against God; for it is not subject to the law of God, neither indeed can be." The apostle, you perceive, couples the hating of God and his law together, as characteristic of every unregenerate man. Then while the heart is thus at enmity with God, the strictest outward morality is nothing in his sight, for he tells us himself, "The Lord looketh on the heart." Thus you perceive, that the doctrine of man's inability to change his own heart, and perform acceptable obedience, is not inconsistent with the fact, that unregenerate men are often moral in their lives.

Con.—But does it not destroy the distinction between right and wrong, to maintain that the moral man does no more to recommend him to God, than the grossly wicked?

Min.—It is not meant that they are both viewed precisely in the same light. Christ commends the Pharisees for their morality, but reproves them for neglecting "the weightier matters of the law, judgment, mercy, and faith;" and tells them, also, that they could not enter into the kingdom of heaven, or be accepted of God, because in all their boasted morality their hearts were not right. All these things ye do, that ye may be seen of men. Verily, I say unto you, ye have your reward. God has so arranged, in his providence and government, that morality and amiability are rewarded. Or, perhaps, it would be better to say, that the reward which we most earnestly seek shall be obtained. The supreme desire of the Pharisees was to obtain a high religious reputation, and they obtained it. They had their reward. If a man wishes to obtain the character of honesty, and gain the confidence of his neighbours, let him pursue the proper course, and he will obtain it—he has his reward. If a child loves his parents, and wishes to retain their affection and confidence, he has but to pursue the proper course, and he obtains it—he has his reward. But still it is true, in all such cases, that "to be seen of men" is the ruling motive, and "God is not in all their thoughts." They would pursue the same course if God had given no law; and as it respects his requirements, their hearts are still in a state of rebellion. They reject Christ, and the authority of God, altogether. And as there are different degrees of punishment in the future world, they may not, perhaps, be "beaten with as many stripes" as the grossly wicked, yet they are equally far from salvation, until the enmity of their hearts is changed, and they are led to the practice of morality and religion from love to God.

This may be illustrated on the simple principles of common justice and common sense. In a gang of pirates we may find many things that are good in themselves. Though they are in wicked rebellion against the laws of the government, they have their own laws and regulations, which they obey strictly. We may find among them courage and fidelity, with many other things that will recommend them as pirates. They may do many things, too, which the laws of the government require, but they are not done because the government has so required, but in obedience to their own regulations. For instance, the government requires honesty, and they may be strictly honest, one with another, in their transactions, and the division of all their spoil. Yet, as it respects the government, and the general principle, their whole life is one of the most wicked dishonesty. Now, it is plain, that whilst they continue in their rebellion they can do nothing to recommend them to the government as citizens. Their first step must be to give up their rebellion, acknowledge their allegiance to the government, and sue for mercy. So all men, in their natural state, are rebels against God; and though they may do many things which the law of God requires, and which will recommend them as men, yet nothing is done with reference to God and his law. But the regulations of society, respect for public opinion, self-interest, their own character in the sight of the world, or some other worldly or wicked motive, reigns supremely; and God, to whom they owe their heart and lives, is forgotten; or, if thought of at all, his claims are wickedly rejected, his counsels spurned, and the heart, in obstinate rebellion, refuses obedience. Now, it is plain, that while the heart continues in this state the man is a rebel against God, and can do nothing to recommend himself to his favour. The first step is to give up his rebellion, repent of his sins, turn to God, and sue for pardon and reconciliation through the Saviour. This he is unwilling to do, until he is made willing. He loves his sins, and will continue to love them, until his heart is changed.

You can now see clearly the force of the passage of Scripture, which you spoke of in our last conversation—"Whatsoever is not of faith is sin"—Rom. xiv. 23. The same truth is stated in Rom. viii. 8—"They that are in the flesh cannot please God." And Heb. xi. 6—"Without faith it is impossible to please him."

Con.—Are we then to conclude that all the good actions of unregenerate men are sins?

Min.—They are not positively sinful in themselves, but sinful from defect. They lack the principle which alone can make them righteous in the sight of God. In the case of the pirates it is easy to see that all their actions are sin against the government. While they continue pirates, their sailing, mending, or rigging their vessel, and even their eating and drinking, are all sins in the eyes of the government, as they are only so many expedients to enable them to continue their piratical career, and are parts of their life of rebellion. So with sinners. While the heart is wrong, it vitiates everything in the sight of God, even their most ordinary occupations; for the plain, unequivocal language of God is, "The ploughing of the wicked is sin." Prov. xxi. 4.

Con.—This places all men, by nature, in a very dreadful condition—their whole life being nothing but sin—a "treasuring up of wrath against the day of wrath"—and no ability to help themselves.

Min.—It places them entirely dependent upon the sovereign grace and mercy of their offended God. And this, according to the Bible, is their true condition. Such exhibitions of the true state of mankind are, I know, offensive to unregenerate men generally; and many have tried to find out a system of doctrines more palatable to the popular mind. But all such attempts are unfaithful to God, and the souls of men. That teacher of religion has but a poor errand to the sacred desk who attempts thus to "sew pillows under the arms" of his hearers, as Ezekiel describes the effeminate teachers in his day. It is an attempt to heal the hurt of the sinner slightly, and crying peace, where there is no peace. His lost, ruined, and helpless state needs to be constantly set before him; and until he is brought to feel it, he will never seek help where alone it is to be found.

Con.—But as the sinner's inability consists in his wicked love of sin, and unwillingness to love God, has he not some power over his will, that might be exercised in determining his choice of God and holiness?

Min.—I have already remarked, that the will in choosing is influenced by motives, and the motives preponderate according to the state of the heart, or moral taste. But, perhaps, it would be useful for us to look at this a little further, before proceeding to the arguments drawn from the Bible respecting man's inability; both of which we will consider at any time you may have leisure.

DIALOGUE XI.

FREE WILL.

Minister.—The doctrine which we proposed to consider this evening, namely, the powers of the will, is one that involves a great many abstruse questions, which it would not, perhaps, be expedient to enter upon largely at present. But I will endeavour to give you a plain, common sense view of it, if I can, without any metaphysical subtleties.

Convert.—You spoke at our last interview of an inability of will; but is this consistent with freedom of will? Is not the will capable of acting freely, and of choosing what it pleases?

Min.—Certainly; but this is not the question at issue. It is admitted on all hands that the will is free, and does choose what it pleases. But the question is, whether the will has power to choose contrary to what it pleases, or anything that is in direct opposition to what it does choose. It is admitted on all hands that choice is made according to the highest pleasure, or strongest inclination; and the point to be considered is, whether it has power to choose, in direct hostility to its strongest inclinations, and whether these strongest inclinations do not always operate in determining choice.

Con.—But do not men often choose that which is contrary to their desires and inclinations?

Min.—They often choose what is in some respects disagreeable; but there is always some other motive, which at the time influences the choice, which in other circumstances would not be made. For instance, a man may and can eat wormwood, but he will not do it, unless there be some inducement presented, which influences his choice in so doing, and makes it, for the time, his strongest inclination. But then the question still remains, while his ruling inclination, or pleasure, continues to choose as it does, that which, upon the whole, seems most desirable, is there any faculty or power in the will to act contrary?—that is, is there any cause adequate to the production of such an effect? There can be no effect without an adequate cause; and when there is a cause adequate to the production of an effect, there must be some greater cause to prevent that effect, or to produce its opposite.

Now, it is admitted on all hands, that motives and inclinations are the causes which operate, in producing the acts of the will in choosing and refusing; and that the will always does act in the way in which the strongest inclinations lead. But it is still contended by the advocates of the human ability scheme, that there is in the will a power to choose in opposition to its strongest inclination. But where is their proof? They admit, that though there is such a power, it never acts. Then it is admitted, that it is not a cause adequate to the production of the effect. Why, then, contend for it? Of what use is it? It produces no effects in morals or religion It only serves the purpose of some philosophizing theologians, to bolster up their system, which they find cannot stand without it. But let us look at it. A man in certain circumstances, with motives operating without, and inclinations within, is induced to act in a certain way. He chooses that to which his strongest inclinations lead him. Here are cause and effect. Now, if under the same circumstances, and with the same inclinations, his will has a power to choose the contrary of what it does, he either makes the choice, or he does not. If he makes the contrary choice, then his will chooses contrary to what it does choose, which is a self-contradiction. If he does not make the contrary choice, then there is no cause adequate to the production of the effect, and the power of the will to choose contrary to its choice amounts to just nothing at all.

Con.—But might he not choose otherwise if the will were so inclined?

Min.—Certainly; but that is not the point. I am endeavouring to show you, that it always does act as it is inclined; but the point is, has it power to choose contrary to its choice, whether it be inclined or not, and in spite of all opposing inclinations? Scales will turn in an opposite direction, if there be a preponderating weight—a cause adequate to the effect—but without it they will not. No more will the will act in opposition to its strongest inclinations and motives. The cause in the one case is just as adequate to the production of the effect as in the other.

Thus, the faculty of will, in good and bad men, exerts their volitions; but the character of these volitions is determined under given motives, not by the natural faculty itself, abstractly considered, but by the moral state of the heart; and if it be in a certain moral state, it cannot be a property of the will to put forth choices of an opposite moral character, for it is admitted that the heart always rules the choices of the will; and consequently, you perceive, we are brought back to our former conclusion, that man in his natural state is unable to love God, and put forth holy exercises, because his strongest inclinations and desires lead in an opposite direction. He is wickedly unwilling, and therefore unable. He chooses sin deliberately and freely, and always will until a gracious change is wrought by the Spirit of God. "Verily, verily, I say unto thee, except a man be born again he cannot see the kingdom of God."—John iii. 3.

Con.—But when motives are presented, and the will chooses or refuses, according to the moral state of the inner man, without any power in itself to put forth choices contrary to that moral state, is the doctrine not liable to objection, on the ground that the motives are often presented under circumstances over which the man has no control?

Min.—It is true that the motives are furnished in the providence of God. The murderer is kept in life, in God's providence, and is indebted to God for strength to kill his victim, and also for the opportunity. Joseph's brethren could not have cast him into the pit, or sold him, if it had not been so arranged in the providence of God that he was sent to them. In this way they were furnished with the external motive. And I know the objection is urged, that if God furnish the motives, he is in this sense the author of sin. But of all the objections of errorists, this is among the most silly, that because God places man in circumstances, and gives him opportunities to do good, because he chooses to pervert them to evil purposes, God is, therefore, blamable with his sin.

A man makes a musical instrument, with the design that it may delight him with its sweet, harmonious sounds; and when it is made he finds it "good." It answers the purposes for which it was designed perfectly; but from some cause it becomes damaged, and then, under the same process which formerly produced harmony, there is now nothing but discord. Now, it is plain, that though he is the author of the sound, he is not the author of the discord. That arises from the defect of the instrument. And for certain reasons that may operate, he may keep it in order externally, and touch its strings, knowing that it will produce discord, and still not be the author of it. So God keeps in order the system of the world, in all its various operations of life and action; and his providence with men is all so arranged, that if they were holy, the external motives he presents would at all times produce good results. Had not Joseph's brethren indulged a wicked hatred toward him, his coming to them would have afforded an opportunity of doing good to him and their aged father. But their wicked hearts perverted it into an occasion of evil.

Con.—But does not this doctrine of inability tend to make sinners more careless? Will they not say, that as they cannot change their own hearts, all efforts to seek God, and all striving after holiness are useless?

Min.—I believe it has just the opposite tendency. It is because the sinner does not feel his lost and helpless condition, that he remains careless. There is not a careless sinner in the world, who is not a full believer in the doctrine of perfect ability. It is his resolution to repent and turn to God at some future time, that keeps him easy; and he feels perfectly competent to the task. He has no sense whatever of his absolute dependence upon God. He believes that it is something that he can attend to at any time, and at some convenient time he will do it.

And just in proportion as you strengthen that belief, you increase his carelessness, and lull him to sleep on the awful brink of eternal ruin. It is only when he is brought to feel his entire helplessness, and dependence upon sovereign grace, that he will seek help where it is to be found. Then, and not till then, will he rejoice in the truth, that his "help is laid upon one who is mighty to save." It is the hiding of this wholesome truth that has tended to make so many fitful professors of religion, and made religion with many to consist in a kind of spasmodic or occasional action. They are taught, that if they purpose to serve God, that is all the change they need; and that this is as easily done as to raise the hand. They may, and often do, change the outward purpose; but if the heart be not changed by divine grace, they will be sure to change back again. "He that striveth for the mastery, is not crowned, unless he strive lawfully." And the only lawful way for a sinner to strive, is with a feeling of dependence on God, and with the earnest prayer, "Create in me a clean heart, O God; and renew a right spirit within me."

Con.—I believe it is always best for us all to know the worst of our spiritual condition.

Min.—Let us now look at what the Bible says on the doctrine of inability. And I would remark, in the first place, that the doctrine is plainly taught in all those passages which speak of the necessity of regeneration. John iii. 3—"Except a man be born again, he cannot see the kingdom of God"—and 7—"Marvel not that I said unto thee, ye must be born again"—with many other passages, which I need not enumerate.

Again, it is taught in all those passages which ascribe this work directly to the Spirit of God. John iii. 5—"Except a man be born of water and of the Spirit, he cannot see the kingdom of God." Acts xvi. 14—"The Lord opened her heart, that she attended to the things which were spoken of Paul." 1 Thess. i. 5—"Our gospel came not unto you in word only, but in power, and in the Holy Ghost." 1 Cor. 3, 6, and 7—"I have planted, Apollos watered, but God gave the increase. So, then, neither is he that planteth anything, neither he that watereth, but God that giveth the increase." Phil. ii. 13—"It is God that worketh in you, both to will and to do." Ezek. xxxvi. 26 and 27—"A new heart also will I give you, and a new Spirit will I put within you; and I will take away the stony heart out of your flesh, and I will give you a heart of flesh. And I will put my Spirit within you, and cause you to walk in my statutes." John i. 13—"Which were born not of blood, nor of the will of the flesh, nor of the will of man, but of God." But I need not enumerate further. The Bible everywhere ascribes the work of producing holiness in the heart of a sinner, to the direct agency of God. And there is not a single word or passage which ascribes it to the sinner himself.

Con.—I do not recollect ever to have seen or heard it asserted, that any passage of Scripture directly asserts that the sinner is the agent in his own change of heart: but it is inferred from the fact that he is commanded to do it.

Min.—That argument is based upon the false assumption, that there is nothing duty, which there is not full ability to perform; the absurdity of which, I think, I clearly showed you in our last conversation. But let us look at those passages of the Bible, which assert the doctrine of inability in plain and unequivocal language. John vi. 44—"No man can come to me, except the Father which has sent me, draw him." Eph. ii. 1—"You hath he quickened, who were dead in trespasses and sins." 1 Cor. ii. 14—"The natural man receiveth not the things of the Spirit of God, for they are foolishness unto him; neither can he know them, because they are spiritually discerned." Rom. viii. 7 —"The carnal mind is enmity against God: for it is not subject to the law of God, neither indeed can be." These, with other passages, quoted in our former conversation, "They that are in the flesh, cannot please God," &c., present the doctrine in language that cannot be softened down, without destroying their sense altogether.

DIALOGUE XII.

EFFECTUAL CALLING.

Convert.—Since our last conversation, I have been reflecting on the views you presented respecting human ability, and feel constrained to believe, that man in his natural state is not able of himself to change his own heart. Indeed, it is so plain a truth, that I now rather wonder that it should be controverted by any one who has thoroughly considered the subject. I find even the "Doctrinal Tracts" of the Methodist church, teach it in plain language. On page 134, it is said, that "no sinner can believe, but by the almighty power of God." But I find it also stated in the same connection, that God gives to all men "sufficient grace" to enable them to believe, and consequently "their death lies at their own door." And, my Methodist neighbour contends, that if this were not done, God could not be sincere in offering salvation to all men.

Minister.—That is the most common doctrine of those who reject the doctrines of grace, respecting regeneration, effectual calling &c.: and, you might have observed, that the "Doctrinal Tracts," in the same connection, teach that this is necessary, not only "to maintain the sincerity of God," but also "to vindicate his equity at the great day, in condemning the impenitent." I am at a loss to know, how any amount of grace short of regeneration, can be called "sufficient." If it does not change the sinner's moral tastes and inclinations, it is not sufficient to enable him to believe and repent. How can he repent of sin, when he still loves it? There never was, and never will be, a single instance of a true penitent, whose heart is unchanged. I need not stay to prove, that God does not give "sufficient grace to all men," in this sense. The outward calls of the gospel are gracious, but no one except those who deny the operations of the Spirit altogether, will contend that this is "sufficient." The movements of the Spirit, which many experience in conviction, are gracious, but all admit that these are not "sufficient." What could we think of a teacher of religion, who would tell a sinner under conviction, that he had grace enough, and need not look for more! And, the fact of telling him to pray for more, and of praying for such an one that he might have more given him, is sufficient proof that it is not deemed "sufficient." If this be what is meant by "sufficient grace," it is calling that sufficient which is not sufficient; and, if they mean any other kind of grace, I know not what kind it is.

Con.—It seems to me contrary to all Christian experience, to maintain that any kind or degree of grace, is sufficient to lead a sinner to Christ, short of that which changes his heart, and gives him new views and feelings.

Min.—But you have not yet seen the worst feature of this doctrine of "sufficient grace to all men." It is based upon the assumption, that without bestowing this grace, God could not be sincere in offering salvation, or just in condemning unbelievers. Then he was bound to save all the human family without an atonement. For, if it would be unjust in him to condemn them, it would be just to save them, and whatever is strict justice, he is bound by every perfection of his nature to do. Then, without the atonement, and this "sufficient grace," all men would be saved. But God has provided a Saviour, and gives this "sufficient grace," to make it consistent with his justice to condemn some, who do not believe. This not only makes God the author of sin, but it makes him the author of the eternal death of every impenitent sinner. I do not suppose, that the abettors of the doctrine intend to teach a sentiment so grossly blasphemous, but the conclusion is legitimate and necessary. If what they teach be true, this must be true likewise.

The same doctrine is taught in different language on page 154, of the "Doctrinal Tracts." "The moment Adam fell, he had no freedom of will left; but God, when of his own free grace he gave the promise of a Saviour, to him and his posterity, graciously restored to mankind a liberty and power to accept of proffered salvation." Now, if there were no freedom of will there could be no accountability. It is a plain dictate of common sense, that a man is not accountable for anything he does not do willingly and freely. Then, where there is no freedom of will, there can be no sin. But God gave them a freedom of will to capacitate them to sin. Hence, all mankind are sinners by the grace of God! But I need not follow further the absurdities of such doctrines. They are all only miserable shifts to get clear of the doctrines of grace, and to fix up some scheme that will lead the helpless sinner away from his entire dependence on the free, unmerited, sovereign grace of God.

Con.—But, is this clearly reconcilable with the commands and exhortations of the Bible to come to Christ, which I have heard Presbyterian ministers urge as strenuously upon sinners, as any other class of preachers?

Min.—It is the duty of the sinner to strive; and, to those who do so, God has given gracious promises. But, they should always be taught to strive with a feeling of dependence, and earnest looking to God for grace. This is the course marked out in the word of God. "Work out your own salvation with fear and trembling, for it is God that worketh in you both to will and to do of his good pleasure." You perceive, that the apostle, instead of making the dependence of the sinner an excuse for doing nothing, makes it the ground of his encouragement to work. There is no language in our Confession of Faith more forcible or comprehensive than this. God works in us "both to will and to do;" and, thereupon, the apostle bases his exhortation to "work out our salvation." And, "what God hath joined together, let no man put asunder." Let these things always be kept in mind, and followed out, and there is no danger of mistake in going too far on either hand. No one can err in striving too earnestly for salvation, if it be done in the right way. No more can any one err, at the same time, in casting himself upon God, with too much dependence and earnest prayer for grace. Hence, boasting is excluded by the law of faith; and every true Christian is prepared to say, "By the grace of God I am what I am." This, however, could not be the case, if any part of the work of regeneration were his own. "Who maketh thee to differ?" is the emphatic inquiry of the apostle on this subject; and, let any one who thinks he has had any part in his own regeneration, answer the question if he can, in accordance with the language of the Bible.

You can now see the truth of the language of our catechism, when it says, "We are made partakers of the redemption purchased by Christ, by the effectual application of it to us by his Holy Spirit." And further, "The Spirit applieth to us the redemption purchased by Christ, by working faith in us, and thereby uniting us to Christ, in our effectual calling." And, again, "Effectual calling is the work of God's Spirit, whereby convincing us of our sin and misery, enlightening our minds in the knowledge of Christ, and renewing our wills, he doth persuade and enable us to embrace Jesus Christ, freely offered to us in the Gospel." Shorter Catechism—answer to questions 29, 30, 31. This language any one may compare with Scripture. Rom. viii. 30—"Whom he did predestinate, them he also called, and whom he called, them he also justified." 2 Thess. ii. 13—"God hath from the beginning chosen you to salvation, through sanctification of the Spirit and belief of the truth." 2 Cor. iii. 3—"The epistle of Christ ministered by us, written, not with ink, but with the Spirit of the living God, not in tables of stone, but in fleshly tables of the heart." 2 Tim. i. 9—"Who hath saved us, and called us with an holy calling, not according to our works, but according to his own purpose and grace." Ezek. xxxvi. 26—"A new heart also will I give you, and a new spirit will I put within you," &c. Ezek. xi. 19—"I will give them one heart, and I will put a new spirit within you." Psa. cx. 3—"Thy people shall be willing in the day of thy power." Eph. ii. 1—"You hath he quickened who were dead in trespasses and sins." Verse 5—"Even when we were dead in sins, hath quickened us together with Christ, (by grace ye are saved.)" Verse 8—"By grace are ye saved through faith, and that not of yourselves, it is the gift of God." But, I need not enumerate further, though it would be easy to find hundreds of texts which teach the same truth. The Bible, you perceive, teaches abundantly the doctrine of "sufficient grace," but it is in a sense very different from that taught in the "Doctrinal Tracts." The sufficient grace of the Bible is that which finds man "dead in trespasses and sins, calls him with a holy calling, gives him a new heart, makes him willing, quickens him unto life, and leads him to Christ"—or, as our Catechism expresses it, "persuades and enables him to embrace Jesus Christ." It is in this sense that "faith is the gift of God;" and, indeed, this is the only conceivable sense in which it can be.

Con.—But does not the doctrine of "sufficient grace to all men," meet, in the most satisfactory manner, the objection, that God is partial in giving more grace to some than to others?

Min.—Even if it did, we are not bound to adopt it, when it is so plainly contradicted by the Bible. I believe, however, that this is the ground upon which it is based. Men are unwilling to allow God his sovereignty, either in providence or mercy. And when the Bible tells us he distinguishes in his dealings with man, they reject the doctrine, and call it partiality in

God to give anything more to one than to another; and leaving the plain doctrine of revelation, endeavour to patch up a scheme of their own, which they boast of as vindicating the character of God, when, in fact, it robs him of his sovereignty. But still their scheme, instead of relieving, increases the difficulty.

Con.—How does it increase the difficulty? If God gives to all men the same amount of grace, there surely can be no charge of partiality.

Min.—There would still be the same ground for the charge, unless he would go further, and place all men precisely in the same circumstances, and give them precisely the same dispositions, that, according to this scheme, all might have precisely the same opportunities of improving their equal amount of grace. Similar causes operating in similar circumstances, must invariably produce similar effects. The amount of grace that is "sufficient" to lead one man to the Saviour, will invariably lead another of the same disposition, placed in similar circumstances. And if all men possessed the same dispositions, and were in the same circumstances, what is sufficient for one would be for another, and all would be saved. But all are not in the same circumstances, and have not the same opportunities. Some are born of Christian parents, whose instructions and prayers are blessed to their conversion. Others are taught from their infancy to disobey God and contemn religion. Some never hear of a Saviour, or of the true God. Now, over these circumstances, they themselves have no control; and those who accuse God of partiality because he discriminates in grace, and contend that it would be injustice to bestow more upon one man than another, are bound to explain, upon the same principles, the facts of his providence, by which he orders the lots of men in the world. But here they will find an insuperable difficulty, because they cannot deny the fact, that some are placed in circumstances better calculated to result in their salvation, than others.

How much more consistent with common sense, and with the disposition we ought to exercise toward God and his word, to take the simple language of the Bible, that "he has mercy on whom he will have mercy" and will have trophies of his grace out of all nations and classes of men. And whenever any one turns aside from the truth of the Bible, to reconcile what, in the pride of opinion, he conceives to be difficulties, he will only find himself surrounded with difficulties still more perplexing and insuperable.

Con.—It seems to me a fact that cannot be disputed, that God distinguishes both in his providence and grace, and the objection of partiality, I perceive, amounts to a denial of his sovereign right to do as he pleases, which the Bible everywhere ascribes to him, and which it must be impious to controvert, either directly or indirectly.

But there is another point upon which I wish to have your views, about which I have felt some difficulty; I mean the doctrine of perfect sanctification in this life. I feel that I am very far from what I should be, and my desire is to get clear of all sin. We are commanded in the Bible to "be perfect;" and yet I know your church holds that absolute perfection is not attainable in this life. I feel that it is a question of great practical importance, and would like to have all the information I can derive from every source.

Min.—Call at any time you find convenient, and I will endeavour to give you a plain, scriptural view of it, both as it respects our duty and privilege.

DIALOGUE XIII.

SINLESS PERFECTION.

Minister.—The doctrine we proposed to examine this evening, viz: Whether any one in this life ever attains to absolute sinless perfection, is thus plainly expressed in our Confession of Faith: "No mere man, since the fall, is able in this life perfectly to keep the commandments of God, but doth daily break them, in thought, word, and deed."—Shorter Catechism, Ans. to Qu. 82. I need not stay to prove, that "the commandments of God" are our standard of holiness, and anything that comes short of a perfect fulfilment of all their requirements, in all respects, is not perfect obedience. And we not only sin in every positive violation of the law, but also in every want of perfect conformity to all its holy requirements. Gal. iii. 10—"Cursed is every one that continueth not in all things which are written in the book of the law to do them." It is a plain dictate of common sense, as well as of the Bible, that in failing to do, or to be, what God requires, is sinful, as well as doing, or being, what he forbids. Hence, our Catechism says—"Sin is any want of conformity unto, or transgression of, the law of God."—Shorter Cat. Ans. to Qu. 14.

Convert.—Are we then to account all our infirmities sinful; and all our consequent mistakes and aberrations, whether voluntary or involuntary?

Min.—Everything that is not in strict accordance with God's requirements must be sin. He requires nothing but holiness, and whatever he requires, it is our duty to give. I know it is said by the advocates of the doctrine of perfection, that our infirmities and mistakes are not sinful; and yet, they contradict themselves by saying, that "every such mistake, were it not for the blood of atonement, would expose us to eternal damnation."—"Doctrinal Tracts," p. 311. That is, God would be just in sending us to hell for ever, for that which is not sin! A sentiment more derogatory to God can scarcely be imagined. It is only another attempt to degrade the law of God—to take from it its strictness and spirituality, and bring it down to the low and common views entertained of it by men of the world. It is too generally lost sight of in the world, that the law of God, in its holy requirements, extends to the feelings of the heart, the thoughts, and exercises of the inner man; and errorists almost uniformly fall in with the feelings of the world, and make the law of God a matter of such small moment, that perfect obedience is comparatively easy. But the Bible speaks in different language. What it mainly insists upon, is right feelings and dispositions; and it chiefly condemns feelings and dispositions that are wrong, because from these proceed all the outward conduct. "Out of the heart," says Christ, "proceed evil thoughts, adulteries, murders," &c. And Solomon says, "Keep thy heart with all diligence, for out of it are the issues of life." Love is a feeling, repentance is a feeling, faith is an inward exercise of the soul, humility is a feeling, hope, patience, resignation, charity, meekness, kindness, contentment, &c., are all feelings. Yet who that reads the Bible carefully, does not perceive that all these are required as indispensable duties? And on the other hand, enmity to God is a feeling, unbelief is a feeling, selfishness, pride, impenitence, love of the world, covetousness, envy, anger, hatred, revenge, &c., are all feelings, and all are forbidden as the worst of sins. Hence, it is evident, that to form anything like a proper estimate of our character in the sight of God and his law, we must first and chiefly have respect to the feelings and dispositions of the heart. And before we can be perfect, we must in all these respects, be absolutely and entirely free from the least failure, and exercise all those feelings as purely as the angels in heaven.

Con.—In that case, I do not believe that any one, who has a proper view of himself, will ever claim to be perfect.

Min.—It is, I believe, generally claimed on the ground of perfect love. They claim to have perfect love; and, as the apostle says, "love is the fulfilling of the law," therefore, they are perfect. But any one who thinks he has as much love as he ought to have, has very grovelling ideas of his obligations to God, or very superficial views of himself. But there are other classes of sins, which are rather consequent upon those of the heart and feelings, of which we must take account in forming a proper estimate of our character in the sight of God and his law. The Bible says, that vain, trifling, and foolish thoughts are sinful. Christ classes "evil thoughts" with "thefts, murder, adultery," &c. "The wicked" is not only commanded to "forsake his ways," but also "the unrighteous man his thoughts." Again, we are told, that "the thoughts of the wicked are an abomination unto the Lord," &c. And

God says, in another place—"Hear, O earth, I will bring evil upon this people, even the fruit of their thoughts." Indeed, the character of the man seems to be in some measure determined by his thoughts. "For as a man thinketh in his heart, so is he." These passages, with many others that might be quoted, prove very clearly, that much sin is committed in thought. And if vain and foolish thoughts are sinful, we may not only ask, who is perfect?—but, who can enumerate the sins of a single day? We should remember, too, that thoughts are the language of spirits, and each one has a tongue in the ear of God. Christ answered the thoughts of those around him, as if they had spoken. It is no wonder that God says, "every imagination of the thoughts of man's heart, is evil continually." But this is not all, yet. We must also take into the account, the sins of our tongues. And here I need not speak of falsehood, slander, profanity, &c. These, all know and admit to be sins. But Christ says, that "every idle word, which men shall speak, they shall give account thereof in the day of judgment." Mere idle words, then, are sins, and——

Cor.—But what are idle words?

Min.—All that are not necessary, and that do not tend to produce some good result. The commands of the Bible are, "Let no corrupt communication proceed out of your mouth, but that which is good, to the use of edifying;" "let your speech be always with grace, that it may minister grace to the hearers;" "nor foolish talking, nor jesting, which are not convenient, but rather giving of thanks." These rules may be thought too strict, by the advocates of perfection, but they are the rules which God lays down in his word, by which we are to order our conversation. Every word which does not comport with these rules, is an "idle word," and sinful in the sight of God. Then, where is the man who will stand up before God and say, that in this respect alone, he is free from sin?

But still more: When we take into the account our actions in general, the mountain rises still higher. Here I need not go further than to speak of our sins of omission. The command is, "Withhold not good from him to whom it is due, when it is in the power of thine hand to do it, for to him that knoweth to do good and doeth it not, to him it is sin." From this it is plain, that whenever we have an opportunity of doing good, either to the souls or bodies of others, and neglect to improve it, we sin both against our fellow-men and against God. But further: God tells us,

"Whether ye eat or drink, or whatsoever ye do, do all to the glory of God." This applies to all our words and actions, and proves beyond controversy, that every word we speak, and every action we perform, which is not done with a view to promote the glory of God, is sinful. Of how many sins, then, are we guilty? And where is the perfect man, in this respect? Again: we are commanded to "pray without ceasing," to "rejoice in the Lord always," &c. Every moment that we have not a holy, prayerful frame of mind, we sin. It is admitted on all hands, that it is a sin to swear profanely; but few reflect that it is also a sin not to pray, whenever it is our duty or privilege. But I need not enlarge, though much more might be said in contrasting the obedience of the best men, with the high and holy requirements of the law of God. Enough has been said, however, to show you the truth of the language of our Confession, that "we daily break the commandments of God in thought, word, and deed."

Con.—As it respects the simple fact, that all men are sinners, and that, in this life, no one ever attains to such a degree of perfection in holiness as to be entirely free from sin, I think it cannot be controverted, if we allow the law of God, in all its holy requirements, to be our standard. Indeed, I have never had much difficulty in my mind as to the fact, that all come far short of perfect holiness in this respect. But how are we to understand the commands of God requiring this perfection, if it be not attainable?

Min.—The fact that it is unattained, and unattainable, does not arise from God, but from ourselves, and therefore it is no less our duty, and it should be the constant aim of every Christian. Indeed, no true Christian can rest satisfied with himself, while he feels any remaining corruption, and consequently the warfare is still continued; and, as the Bible expresses it, he goes on "from strength to strength." His standard of holiness is God himself, of whose character the law is a transcript. With the command before him, "Be ye holy, for I the Lord your God am holy," he finds no place to stop short of this, until, like the angels in heaven, he reflects fully and perfectly the image of his Maker.

Con.—But are there not some passages of Scripture, which favour the idea that some are perfect, or that perfection has been attained in this life by some?

Min.—We are told to "mark the perfect man, and behold the upright, for the end of that man is peace." Paul says, "Let us therefore, as many as be perfect, be thus minded," &c. "Be perfect, be of good comfort,"&c. Noah, we are told, "was a just man and perfect," &c. But it is plain, from the connection in which the word is used in other places, that it does not mean an entire freedom from all sin. The primary signification of the original word, which Paul uses in his exhortation to the Corinthians, "be perfect," is collecting together the disjointed or broken parts of a body or system, so as to make it uniform or complete, and that no part be wanting, and there is such a thing attainable, and often attained, as perfection, in this sense: that is, a perfect gospel character. For instance, if a professor of religion be in the habit of prevarication, or if he be covetous or niggardly in his dealings, or in any way exhibits to the world traits of character inconsistent with his profession, they are blots in his Christian character which cast a shade over the whole, and excite doubts as to the reality of his piety. In this respect, every Christian should and can be perfect: that is, he should exhibit the Christian character complete in all its parts. But to love God as much as we should, to exercise constant faith, in all the strength and unwavering confidence that he requires, to have hope, repentance, humility, and all the Christian graces and virtues in constant perfect operation, and to be entirely free from sin in the sight of God, is a very different matter. The Saviour evidently uses the term "perfect" in the former sense, when speaking to the young ruler—"If thou wilt be perfect, go sell all that thou hast," &c. Surely he did not mean, that thereby he would be free from all sin. Perfection, then, in the Bible sense, means integrity, sincerity in our profession, unfeigned love to God, and respect to all his commands. But as our time will not permit us to enter fully into the Bible arguments on this subject, we will defer it to our next interview.

DIALOGUE XIV.

SINLESS PERFECTION.

Conv.rt.—Your views of the sinfulness of all men in the sight of God, presented at our last interview, cannot, I think, be objected to, except on the ground that it is discouraging to the Christian to know that his desires cannot be accomplished, until he ends his earthly career. It must be the most earnest desire of every true Christian to be free from all sin; and will it not have a tendency to paralyze his efforts to grow in grace, to know that his whole life is to be spent in endeavours to attain to that state of perfection which none ever find?

Minister.—I believe it has just the opposite tendency, judging both from the Bible and all Christian experience. Would it be discouraging to a man on a journey, to know that the object he had in view was to be obtained only at the end of it? It would tend to encourage him all the way, to know certainly that he would finish his journey, and there, and there only he would obtain the object he had in view. The way might be long and the journey difficult, but the certain prospect of gaining the desired object would still cheer him in his toil. So Paul expresses his experience, Phil. iii. 13, 14—"Forgetting those things which are behind, and reaching forth unto those things which are before, I press toward the mark, for the prize of the high calling of God in Christ Jesus." This is very far from the language of a Perfectionist. He counted all his former good works and attainments in sanctification only worthy of being forgotten, in comparison with those that were yet before him. But how eagerly he presses forward, knowing that the prize was yet before him, encouraged with the hope which animates every Christian, that perfect meetness for heaven, and release from the world, will be found in immediate connection.

It is, moreover, the desire of every Christian to grow in grace, and while he finds himself advancing in holiness, and growing in conformity to the image of God, he finds in this his greatest encouragement to press on still toward the high and glorious prize that is before him, perfect holiness and perfect happiness in heaven. Perfect happiness must always be an immediate consequence of perfect holiness; and how could Paul say he was pressing on to obtain the prize, if he had already obtained it? In this way, the doctrine of perfection is destructive of growth in grace. A low standard is set up as the mark of Christian attainment; and when any one entertains so good an opinion of himself as to think he has arrived at it, all further advancement is at an end. Such an one must conclude that he has attained to that which the apostle, in his burning zeal, felt himself wanting. And I can only say, that I think a person who sets up this claim, has yet room to make considerable advancement in the grace of humility.

Con.—It has always struck me unfavourably, to hear any one claiming to be perfect; but knowing that the grace of God is all powerful, and that freedom from all sin must be the desire of every Christian, I found difficulty in deciding that no one obtained the blessing. But in looking at the high standard of holiness which the Bible has set up, I think every one, who has a proper view of himself, will decide with the apostle, that it is a "prize of the high calling of God in Christ Jesus," which is yet far before him.

Min.—Let us now look more particularly at some arguments from the Bible. James speaks the language of Christian experience, when he says, James iii. 2—"In many things we offend all." After thus stating the general truth, that "all" are sinners "in many things," he goes on to speak of particular offences, which cast a stain upon the Christian character, and I think plainly teaches the doctrine of Christian perfection, in the sense in which I spoke of it at our last interview, that is, a perfectly consistent gospel character, exhibiting to the world the piety and integrity of the inner man, and the sincerity of his profession. "If any man offend not in word, the same is a perfect man, and able to bridle the whole body," &c. He teaches the same doctrine in chapter i. verse 27—"Pure religion and undefiled before God and the Father is this, to visit the fatherless and widows in their affliction, and to keep himself unspotted from the world." Paul says, Phil. iii. 12—"Not as though I had already attained, either were already perfect." In whatever sense he uses the word here, it is plain that he did not consider himself perfect.

Con.—But are we to suppose that Paul did not maintain a perfect gospel character?

Min.—So far as we know, he did; but if he here uses the word in that sense, it only shows, what is always the fact, that the true Christian, who is striving after holiness, and endeavouring to "let his light shine," feeling his own failures, always puts a worse estimate on his own character, than others who cannot see him as he sees himself. A man who advances in any degree near perfection in this sense, in the eyes of others, will always be found the last man to claim it for himself. In what a striking contrast, then, the language of the apostle appears, to that of our modern boasting Perfectionists! But further, Solomon in his prayer at the dedication of the temple, recorded in 1 Kings viii. 46, beseeches God to be merciful to the sins of his people, and expressly says, "For there is no man that sinneth not." Again, Job ix. 30, 31—"If I wash myself with snow water, and make my hands never so clean; yet shalt thou plunge me into the ditch, and mine own clothes shall abhor me. For he is not a man, as I am, that I should answer him, and we should come together in judgment." Here it is plainly taught, that however pure we may be in the eyes of the world, yet with God we are vile and polluted. The same is taught in stronger language still, in chapter xv. 14—"What is man that he should be clean? And he that is born of a woman, that he should be righteous?" But he speaks more explicitly still, in ix. 20—"If I say I am perfect, it shall also prove me perverse." What a commentary on the language of a Perfectionist! Again, Eccl. vii. 20—"For there is not a just man upon earth, that doeth good, and sinneth not." Isa. lxiv. 6—"We are all as an unclean thing, and all our righteousnesses are as filthy rags." These passages in themselves are sufficient to prove, that the Bible does not consider any one perfect in the sense in which Perfectionists claim it. But further still. Christ teaches us to pray, "Forgive us our trespasses," &c. This direction is given for secret prayer, and therefore these "trespasses," for the pardon of which we are to pray, are our own individual sins. And it is also plain, that it was intended for our daily use. The fourth petition in this summary of prayer given for our direction, is, "Give us this day our daily bread," or "give us day by day our daily bread," and the next petition in immediate connection is, "forgive us our trespasses," &c.

It will not, I presume, be denied, that this direction was also intended for Christians. But, if any one be *perfect*, he cannot pray according to the direction of Christ, for he has no sins to be forgiven. Indeed, the prayers of a man who esteems himself perfect, must be short and few, if he may be said to pray at all. He needs no grace to overcome any sinful propensity. "The body of sin and death," which troubled the apostle so much, is with him perfectly sanctified and holy. He, then, needs neither mercy nor grace. But these are by the apostle made the main errand of a believer at a throne of grace. Heb. iv. 16—"Let us therefore come boldly unto the throne of grace, that we may obtain mercy and find grace to help in time of need." But a Perfectionist has no "time of need;" he needs no more "grace" or "mercy;" he has all the grace he needs, and no sins to be forgiven, and consequently has no errand to a "throne of grace."

As to the Christian experience recorded in the Bible, it is anything but perfectionism. The most extensive records are those of David and Paul. And if perfection were to be found anywhere, we might surely expect to find it in the experience of these eminent servants of God. But what is the fact? We find them lamenting their sins and short-comings, recording their earnest longings after more entire conformity to the law of God, and praying for more grace to enable them to advance in the divine life. We find no intimation anywhere that they thought themselves perfect, but everywhere the reverse. Time will not permit us to examine the numerous passages in which they record their sinfulness as their constant experience. But we will look at some of them. Psa. xxv. 11—"For thy name's sake, O Lord, pardon mine iniquity; for it is great." xxxi. 10—"My strength faileth because of mine iniquity, and my bones are consumed." xxxviii. 3, 4, 5—"Neither is there any rest in my bones, because of my sin. For mine iniquities are gone over my head; as an heavy burden, they are too heavy for me. My wounds stink, and are corrupt, because of my foolishness." xl. 12—"For innumerable evils have compassed me about; mine iniquities have taken hold upon me, so that I am not able to look up; they are more than the hairs of mine head, therefore my heart faileth me." This does not look much like perfection; and much more of the same kind might be given. The 119th Psalm is almost one continued confession of failure in duty, and prayer for quickening grace. Verse 5th—"O that my ways were directed to keep thy statutes." 25—"My soul cleaveth unto the dust: quicken thou me according to thy word." 29—"Remove from me the way of lying, and grant me thy law graciously." 32—"I will run the way of thy commandments, when thou shalt enlarge my heart." 81—"My soul fainteth for thy salvation; but I hope in thy word." 96—"I have seen an end of all perfection; but thy commandment is exceeding broad." 123—"Mine eyes fail for thy salvation, and for the word of thy righteousness." 131—"I opened my mouth and panted: for I longed for thy commandments." 176—"I have gone astray like a lost sheep: seek thy servant; for I do not forget thy commandments." All these express the exercises of the pious soul, that feels its short-comings, and longs after greater conformity to the law of God, but they would sound very strange in the mouth of a Perfectionist.

Paul gives his experience in language equally plain, and, if possible, more strong and explicit. Rom. vii. 14—25—"For we know that the law is spiritual; but I am carnal, sold under sin. For that which I do, I allow not: for what I would, that do I not; but what I hate, that do I. If then I do that which I would not, I consent unto the law, that it is good. Now then it is no more I that do it, but sin that dwelleth in me. For I know that in me, (that is, in my flesh,) dwelleth no good thing: for to will is present with me; but how to perform that which is good I find not. For the good that I would, I do not: but the evil which I would not, that I do. Now if I do that I would not, it is no more I that do it, but sin that dwelleth in me. I find then a law, that when I would do good, evil is present with me. For I delight in the law of God after the inward man. But I see another law in my members, warring against the law of my mind, and bringing me into captivity to the law of sin which is in my members. O wretched man that I am! who shall deliver me from the body of this death? I thank God through Jesus Christ our Lord. So then, with the mind I myself serve the law of God, but with the flesh the law of sin." This, in itself, if there were not another passage in the Bible, is sufficient to prove that the apostle was a stranger to anything like sinless perfection.

Con.—But does not this, taking it all together, prove too much, and, therefore, prove nothing? Does not the apostle use language which cannot be true of the Christian?—"I am carnal, sold under sin." Can this be true of any one who is a true believer? He says in another place, of Christians, "Ye are not under the law, but under grace." How, then, can they be "sold under sin?"

Min.—It is a very strong expression, I admit; and those who advocate the doctrine of perfection, have laid hold of it to prove that the apostle is not giving his own experience, but the feelings of a sinner. But the falsity of such a view, is clearly shown in the 22d verse—"I delight in the law of God after the inward man." And he gives the language of a true believer in the 25th verse—"I thank God through Jesus Christ our Lord." It is as impossible to apply this to an unconverted sinner, as the whole passage to a Perfectionist. But the expression, "carnal, sold under sin," is of very easy solution, if we allow the apostle to explain himself, which he does in the verse immediately following—"For that which I do, I allow not," &c. The word "for," connects the two verses, and shows that the one is explanatory of the other. The simple meaning, therefore, is, that he was an unwilling "servant" of his inward propensities, against which he was struggling, and from which he desired to be free, but which he still felt maintaining their power over him, and still "bringing him into captivity." It expresses, in very strong terms, the inward conflict which every Christian experiences and understands. The passage taken together, contains an unanswerable proof that perfection in holiness is not attainable in this life, or at least that the apostle had not attained it when he wrote this account of his experience. And to my mind it is clear, that a Perfectionist, instead of having completed the Christian warfare, has it yet to begin.

Con.—But have we no account of any one in the Bible, who claimed to have attained perfection in holiness?

Min.—Not unless the Pharisee may be so called, who, Christ tells us, "went up to the temple to pray." He claimed to be perfect, even before God. He had no sins to be pardoned, and no grace to ask, in his own estimation; but thanked God that he was so good. "Lord, I thank thee that I am not as other men," &c. Whether he knew in his heart that he was a sinner or not, we are not told, but we know he claimed to be perfect, and wished to be so esteemed. He had no errand to a throne of grace but to enumerate his virtues, and thank God that he had no sin. But it is only another proof of the truth of the saying of John, 1 John i. 8—"If we say that we have no sin, we deceive ourselves, and the truth is not in us."

Con.—But if so much of our nature still remains unsanctified, does it not afford a ground of fear, that it will entirely overcome all our holy purposes and resolutions, and prove the cause of our final apostacy from God and holiness?

Min.—Every Christian no doubt feels, that if the warfare were to be carried on in his own strength, there would be little doubt as to the result. But the fact that they feel their own weakness, teaches them where their strength lies, and it is thus made instrumental in their perseverance in holiness, through divine grace.

But as this involves the general doctrine of perseverance, we will consider it at our next interview.

DIALOGUE XV.

PERSEVERANCE.

Convert.—The sentiment you advanced at our last interview, that the remaining corruptions of our nature are instrumental in our perseverance in holiness, seems to me a paradox, which I cannot fully understand, or reconcile with the doctrines of grace. Does it not make sin one of the means of grace?

Minister.—A person who feels that he is sick, and uses means for his recovery, does not make his sickness instrumental in his restoration. It is his knowledge of his disease, that leads him to the use of proper means. So, if a Christian's sense of his remaining imperfection, lead him to the fountain of grace, in the use of proper means, it does not make his sin a means of grace. I mentioned it, however, as a fact in Christian experience, to show that our imperfection, in this life, was no argument against our final perseverance, but rather in favour of it. Such was Paul's experience, when he says, 2 Cor. xii. 9, 10—

"Most gladly, therefore, will I rather glory in my infirmities, that the power of Christ may rest upon me. * * * For, when I am weak, then am I strong." It was not his weakness, in itself, that was his strength; but feeling his weakness, he was led to look for grace, that he might enjoy its almighty power. Such, I need hardly tell you, is the experience of every Christian, unless we may except the Perfectionist, whose experience in this, as in everything else, differs from that of Paul. When you look at yourself, and realize your short-comings and failures, and how far your heart is, in many respects, from what it should be, does it not lead you, not only to pray for, but to admire and love that grace, which can, and does elevate, refine, and quicken a heart so cold and insensible?

Con.—I can truly say, that such is my experience; and I have often admired the language of one of our hymns:

"Almighty grace! thy healing power,
How glorious—how divine!
That can to life and bliss restore
So cold a heart as mine."

Min.—This is simply what the apostle means by "glorying in infirmity." And it is easy to see how such experience has a tendency to keep the Christian constantly at a throne of grace, where he finds his only hope of perseverance in holiness. This is the ground upon which the doctrine of perseverance is based. It is not of man, but of God. I need not stay to prove, that we are entirely dependent on God for persevering grace. The work of sanctification is his, and his entirely.

Con.—But is not the Christian actively engaged in his own sanctification?

Min.—He "works out his own salvation"—but still "it is God that worketh in him, both to will and to do."—Phil. ii. 12, 13. The Christian grows in grace, but it is God that enables him. His mind concurs in the work; so that he is not only actively, but zealously engaged in it; but it is in striving to obtain that grace, upon which he feels he is entirely dependent. All his exertions and prayers are to this end. But this, instead of proving that his final perseverance depends upon himself, proves the contrary. If, then, the perseverance of Christians in a life of faith and holiness, depends upon God, and any finally and totally apostatize, it must be because God is either unable or unwilling to carry them forward in their Christian course to complete salvation. That he is unable, I presume none will contend—that he is unwilling, will not, I think, be contended by any one who has anything like a proper estimate of his character, as revealed in his word, and exhibited in his providence and grace. He has regenerated, justified, and, in part, sanctified them; he has given them to his Son as trophies of his cross, pardoned all their sins, adopted them as sons and daughters into his family, and the Saviour has prepared mansions for them in heaven. Then, to say that God is unwilling to preserve them, would, it seems to me, be as absurd and blasphemous as to say that he is unable. 1 Thess. iv. 3—"This is the will of God, even your sanctification." If, then, the work be his, and he be both able and willing to perform it, we may conclude it will be done.

Con.—But though God is willing and able to save them, may he not be provoked to withdraw his Spirit, and leave them to final apostacy, as a punishment for their sins?

Min.—God might, it is true, if he saw fit, withdraw his gifts, and the abandoned sinner would have no just cause of complaint. But the question is, will he do it, after all that he has done for him? His gifts were free, and entirely unmerited. There was no compulsion. Neither was there any want of consideration. Men may bestow gifts inconsiderately and rashly, and afterwards find occasion to withdraw them; but God's gifts are bestowed with a full knowledge of all or any difficulties that might arise in the way of their continuance. He knew when he gave them, whether anything would ever require him to withdraw them. If he gave them with a knowledge that he would withdraw them, (which all must admit, if they should ever be withdrawn,) then he acts a part more capricious than men; for no man would bestow a gift when he knew that it would be so abused that he would be compelled to withdraw it. Yet the advocates of the doctrine of "falling from grace," as it is termed, would have us believe, that God regenerates, justifies, pardons, and in part sanctifies, or as some say sanctifies perfectly, those who he knows must bear his wrath in hell for ever. Surely, the advocates of such a doctrine, do not consider what they teach.

Con.—But may we not suppose that his grace is bestowed conditionally: that is, if the Christian improve the gift, it will be continued and increased; but if not, it will be withdrawn?

Min.—That supposition will not relieve the difficulty. Let us suppose that the grace of justification, or pardon, is bestowed conditionally. But a conditional pardon is no pardon at all. If it be suspended on anything to be done, it is not granted—it is only promised. But if a man is not actually pardoned and justified, he is not a Christian. It is not an unregenerated, unjustified sinner, that we say will be enabled by God to persevere, but the true Christian, who is really a child of God, who has actually been justified through faith, one whose heart has been changed by divine grace, who has exercised faith in the merits of Jesus Christ, who truly loves God, feels thankful for the mercy and grace he has received, rejoices to believe that he is pardoned and accepted of God; and yet he is not pardoned, if it only be promised conditionally, and he is not yet at liberty even to hope for heaven. How could we exhort such an one? We could not exhort him to continue in a state of justification; for he is not yet justified. We could not exhort him to continue a Christian; for he is not yet a Christian—the wrath of God is still abiding on him, and he is still in a state of condemnation—the curse is not yet removed.

But there are other difficulties arising from such a supposition. If pardon and justification be suspended upon the condition of perseverance in holiness, they cannot be bestowed on account of the merits of Christ; and thus it is subversive of the main principle of the gospel. How much more consistent with the plain dictates of common sense, to believe, as the Bible tells us, that when a sinner believes and repents, all his sins are actually pardoned, and that, on the ground of the righteousness of Christ, he is justified and accepted as righteous in the sight of God, and is fully reconciled, and adopted as a child of God, and an heir of heaven, and the mansions of glory, to which he will certainly be received.

Con.—Are we, then, to suppose that the perseverance of the Christian is altogether unconditional? That is, are we to suppose that he will certainly obtain complete salvation, whether he live a holy life or not?

Min.—That is supposing a contradiction. It is perseverance in holiness that is secured; and it is secured in the same way with his regeneration and justification. You recollect that when we were considering the doctrine of election, it was made plain from the fact, that God is the author of regeneration and conversion from sin to holiness; because, when God converts a sinner, he does it from design, and as he can have no new designs, it must have been eternal. Now, his design is not to save any one in sin, but "through sanctification of the Spirit and belief of the truth."—2 Thess. ii. 13. His purpose to save embraces both regeneration and sanctification. When you look at God's mercy and grace, in your conversion, and trace it back to its source, you find the doctrine of election; and you have only to trace it forward to its completion, to find the doctrine of perseverance. You have said that God, in your conversion, was fulfilling his gracious design which he must have had toward you. That design was, of course, to save you through the operations of his Spirit, transforming you anew, and making you meet for heaven. Thus, holiness is not a condition of perseverance, but a part of it; and to suppose that it is irrespective of holiness, is a contradiction. Here, too, we see an argument for the truth of the doctrine, which, to my mind, is conclusive. If God's design, in your conversion, were not to save you finally, it could not be a gracious design. When he sent his Spirit to change your heart, and enable you to believe on his Son; raised your affections to himself, and fixed your hopes in heaven, if he only designed to lead you forward for a time, and then leave you to go to hell at last, his design was anything but gracious. But let us suppose such a case. A man, through the grace of God, is converted at thirty years of age. All his sins are pardoned. He is justified, and in part, sanctified, admitted to communion and fellowship with God, rejoices to believe that he is forgiven and accepted of God through the merits of Christ, and is cheered with the prospect of complete salvation. He lives a Christian life for one or two years, "falls from grace," loses entirely all his interest in religion, dies a child of Satan, and goes to hell. How will such an one give his account? The sins of his first thirty years have all been pardoned through Christ. But if he be punished only for the sins of the last few months, he does not receive according to his deeds. His punishment is not in proportion to his guilt, which is contrary to the principles of justice, and the plain declarations of the Bible. But the supposition that any one, who has been truly regenerated and sanctified, washed in the blood of Christ, and adopted as a child of God, will at last be left of God and sent to hell, is so inconsistent with the character and dealings of God, that it only needs to be mentioned to see its absurdity. Yet all this absurdity is involved in the doctrine of "falling from grace."

Con.—But will it not have a tendency to make the Christian feel secure, and relax his efforts to advance in holiness, to know that his salvation is certain and unalterably fixed in the purpose and good pleasure of God?

Min.—It is often urged by the enemies of the doctrine of perseverance, that it is dangerous. It is not uncommon to hear them say, that if the doctrine be true, any one may live as he pleases. I once heard a preacher say: "If I believed such a doctrine, I would care nothing about growth in grace, or living a holy life." But such objectors forget, that if they speak according to their feelings, they give strong evidence that they are strangers to the love of God, and cast a severe reflection upon true religion. Suppose a father, when about to settle a patrimony upon his son, is told that it will be dangerous to do so, lest, when the son should know that all was securely his, he would treat him unkindly. What severer reflection could he cast upon the son? And what mournful evidence it would be of the son's entire selfishness, and want of love to his father, to hear him say, that if his father would fix the patrimony securely in his hands, he would not care how he treated him! Just such is the evidence that the professed

Christian gives of his love to God, who says that if he once felt sure of heaven, he would not care how he lived. I admit that it would be dangerous to make heaven sure to such. Whether it would be dangerous or not, for a father thus to settle the patrimony upon his son, would depend altogether on the nature of the son's feelings towards him. If they were altogether selfish, it would be dangerous. But if the son truly loved his father, it would increase his filial attachment to know that his father had done so much for him. The more he would give the son, the more the son would love him. So, if a Christian have true love to God, we need not fear to tell him how much God has done for him. The more he sees of the love of God, the more his own heart will be warmed with the heavenly flame, and he will desire the more to be conformed to his image. I think it will be admitted, that it is the experience of every Christian, that the brighter and firmer his hopes are of heaven, the more he desires to be made meet for it; and just in proportion as faith is to him the certain "evidence (or confidence) of things not seen," he presses with eagerness "to the mark, for the prize of the high calling of God in Christ Jesus."

The doctrine of perseverance, then, to a

true Christian, is one of his greatest incentives to growth in grace; and every one upon whom it has a contrary effect, has much reason to doubt the reality of his religion. His love to God cannot be sincere. But as our conversation has been sufficiently protracted at present, we will defer the Bible argument on the subject to another time.

DIALOGUE XVI.

PERSEVERANCE.

Convert.—There is one argument against the doctrine of perseverance, drawn from facts, that I have found difficult to meet, or answer. There are many cases of persons who give all the evidences of a change of heart, and seem, for a time, to enjoy all the comforts and blessings of true religion, who return to the world and sin, and become worse than they were before.

Minister.—They thereby prove, in the clearest manner, that their religion was vain. They have not had that sealing of the Holy Spirit, with which he indelibly marks the heirs of grace. I know it is counted uncharitable to say, that all such had only a false hope, and that their house was only built on the sand; and, though by saying so, we come under the anathema of the zealous advocates of the doctrine of "falling from grace," we know we are not the first who have been thus denounced, and will likely not be the last. The doctrine of perseverance was one of the distinguishing doctrines of the Reformation, and met with the bitterest opposition from the Pope and his adherents. The Council of Trent decreed, that "if any person shall say that a man who has been justified cannot lose grace, and that, therefore, he who falls and sins was never truly justified, he shall be accursed." But the denunciations of Papists, and other errorists, cannot affect the truth of a doctrine plainly taught by the Saviour himself. He tells us that many, who had such false hopes, will appear at the day of judgment, to whom he will say, "I never knew you; depart from me, ye that work iniquity."—Matt. vii. 23. Now, if the doctrine of "falling from grace" be true, some at that day could contradict the Judge, and tell him, "You did know me; I was regenerated by your Spirit; I was justified through your righteousness; pardoned through your blood; sanctified by your grace; enjoyed seasons of communion with you; you heard my prayers; called me brother; and I rejoiced that you were 'not ashamed to call me brother,' (Heb. ii. 11,) for I was a true child of God." Now, it is very plain, that all this would be true, if any fall away, totally and finally, who once had true religion; and the saying of the Judge, that he "never knew them," would not be true. But the language of the Saviour plainly teaches, that all professors of religion, who are finally lost, were only false professors, and were entire strangers to true religion. We are thus placed under the necessity of contradicting this plain statement of Christ himself, or of disbelieving that any who are true Christians will finally be lost.

Con.—But are there not other passages of Scripture, which seem to favour the doctrine, that a Christian may totally and finally apostatize, and be eternally lost?

Min.—There are several passages that make such a supposition, from which the advocates of the doctrine think it clearly proved. It is, however, only supposed; it is no where directly asserted: whereas, it is again and again directly asserted, that they shall not fall away. And, it is a plain dictate of common sense, that we should never make a supposition contradict a positive assertion, or give the supposition a preference, to establish a doctrine which contradicts the assertion. There are such suppositions made respecting God himself. The Psalmist, in the eleventh Psalm, speaks of God being the great foundation of his trust and hope, and adds, in the third verse, "If the foundations be destroyed, what can the righteous do?" This is a supposition that God would prove unworthy of our confidence, or should fail in his promises, &c. And the supposition is made to excite our gratitude, in contrasting our privilege of trusting in God, with the wretchedness of our condition, if that foundation were taken away, and we could no longer put our trust in him. Now, who would ever think of taking this supposition to prove the possibility of God failing us, as a rock upon which we may at all times trust with unwavering confidence? And yet, it is just as legitimate a course of reasoning, as to argue from the supposition of the Christian being lost, that he may be. Such suppositions are frequent in the Bible, and they are not intended to teach, that the cases supposed will actually occur; but, as in the case above, to show us the excellence of the opposite truth.

Con.—But are there no positive assertions in the Bible, that Christians do, or may, finally and totally apostatize and perish?

Min.—I have not been able to find a single passage in which it is asserted; and all the passages that I have seen quoted by the abettors of the doctrine, amount to nothing more than suppositions, such as I have mentioned. One passage upon which they rely very much, is Ezek. xxxiii. 13—"When I shall say to the righteous, that he shall surely live; if he trust to his own righteousness and commit iniquity, all his righteousness shall not be remembered; but for his iniquity that he hath committed, he shall die for it." It is supposed, by the most eminent commentators, that the "righteous" here spoken of, are to be understood as those false professors of whom Christ will testify, he never knew them. This understanding of the passage, is rendered more forcible from the fact, that they are warned against "trusting to their own righteousness," which is always a characteristic of the false professor. If that be the import of the term, as here used, it affords no proof, or even a supposition, of the true Christian falling away. But even if we understand by the term "righteous," true Christians, it only amounts to a supposition, or what is termed a hypothetical statement. It contains a two-fold hypothesis: "If he trust to his own righteousness," and if he "commit iniquity." Now it will be admitted, I think, that there is no danger of a true Christian "trusting to his own righteousness." Yet the case is supposed; and because it is supposed, is no proof that he will. Neither is the supposition of his "committing iniquity," so as finally and totally to apostatize, any proof that he will.

But another passage which is always

quoted, and relied on, to prove the doctrine, is Heb. vi. 4, 5, 6—"For it is impossible for those who were once enlightened, and have tasted of the heavenly gift, and were made partakers of the Holy Ghost, and have tasted the good word of God, and the powers of the world to come, if they shall fall away, to renew them again unto repentance." This passage, you perceive, contains a supposition, and a positive assertion based upon it. The supposition is of the Christian "falling away," and the positive assertion is, the impossibility of their being "renewed again unto repentance." But those who plead it as proof that the supposed case may occur, overlook entirely the positive assertion, which directly disproves their whole system. They contend, that a true Christian may fall away entirely, and be renewed again—that a person may be a child of God to-day, and a child of Satan to-morrow, and, again, a child of God the next day. They seem to forget entirely, that almost all these hypothetical statements respecting falling from a state of grace, have coupled with the hypothesis, this positive assertion; so, if these statements prove anything at all respecting their system, it is, that it is false. But they are hypothetical statements, which were not intended to prove, that the cases supposed would actually occur, but to show us the necessity of continuing in holiness to the attainment of final salvation. They are incentives to watchfulness, diligence, and prayer; and thus are the means of our perseverance in grace. God deals with us in this, as in all things else, as rational creatures, and works upon us by means and motives, addressed to our hopes and fears. This, I think, is plain from the context. The apostle, after having given this solemn warning, adds, in the ninth verse, "But beloved, we are persuaded better things of you, and things that accompany salvation, though we thus speak." And then he goes on to speak of the "oath" and "promise" of God, that "we might have a strong consolation, who have fled for refuge to lay hold upon the hope set before us." Thus, upon the supposition that the apostle, in this passage, is speaking of the true Christian, it proves nothing for the Arminian. But I am inclined to believe, that he is speaking of those who, in common language, "have sinned away their day of grace." We know that when a sinner has been visited with a great many warnings, and made the subject of the operations of the Holy Spirit, warning and convincing of sin, if he wickedly resist all, there is a point at which the forbearance and mercy of God will cease, and he will be left to himself, to take the course he has deliberately chosen. And when God says of any one, "let him alone," he is "given up to his own heart's lusts:" for him there is no hope. And though by the word enlightening him, and the Spirit's striving, he has been brought almost into the kingdom, yet he "falls back into perdition." Now it seems to me, that the apostle exactly describes the case of such an one; and all he says may characterize one who has never been truly converted. They were "once enlightened." So are those who hear the gospel, and understand its doctrines: they are not savingly enlightened, but enjoy the light of the gospel in a very important sense. They have "tasted of the heavenly gift." This is true of all God's creatures, and more especially of those who enjoy the blessings of the gospel, and have, to any extent, felt the operations of the Spirit. They were "made partakers of the Holy Ghost." So is every sinner, who has been seriously impressed, in view of his sins and danger. They have "tasted the good word of God." So had the thorny ground and stony ground hearers, in the parable of the sower. They have tasted, also, of the "powers of the world to come." It is difficult to determine what is the precise meaning of this expression. If we are to understand by it, hopes of heaven, thousands have them who are not true Christians. But we can found no argument upon a conjectural interpretation. Then, as any and all these blessings may be enjoyed by those who are not true Christians, it seems to me the most likely the apostle is speaking of such. But be that as it may; the passage, as we have seen, plainly contradicts the Arminian doctrine of falling from grace, and being again renewed. There are other similar passages, but this, I believe, is considered by them as the most conclusive in their favour, and consequently, the doctrine has very little support in the Bible.

Con.—But are there not commands and exhortations, in different parts of the Scriptures, addressed to true Christians, which seem to imply that they are in danger of being lost, if they indulge in sin?

Min.—The fact that God will preserve them, does not supersede the use of all legitimate means to secure the end. His purpose to save them, embraces all the means of its accomplishment. He saves by his word and ordinances, and a diligent improvement of opportunities and privileges. This being his instituted plan of effecting his purpose, exhortations and admonitions do not necessarily imply any uncertainty as to the issue. They only point out the manner and order, in which the design will be accomplished. Paul, in a storm at sea, exhorts the sailors to remain in the ship, and work for their lives, and tells the centurion if *they* went away they would all be lost; but will any one say, that there was in reality any uncertainty as to the issue? God had promised that they should be saved, and his character was at stake. But still, the exhortation of Paul was one principal means of their safety. So the exhortations and warnings addressed to Christians are made the means of their perseverance.

But let us now look at some of the plain declarations of the Bible on this subject. And here I would observe, that we are not compelled to resort to suppositions and inferences, but have plain and positive statements, proving as clearly as language can prove, that true Christians will be preserved to complete salvation. Psa. lxxxix. 30—37 —"If his children forsake my law, and walk not in my judgments: if they break my statutes, and keep not my commandments; then will I visit their transgression with the rod, and their iniquity with stripes. Nevertheless my loving kindness will I not utterly take from him, nor suffer my faithfulness to fail. My covenant will I not break, nor alter the thing that is gone out of my lips. Once have I sworn by my holiness, that I will not lie unto David. His seed shall endure for ever, and his throne as the sun before me. It shall be established for ever as the moon, and as a faithful witness in heaven." In this psalm, as in many others, David is made to personify Christ. This is plain from verse 27, and other parts—"I will make him my first-born, higher than the kings of the earth." In the 19th verse, God says—"I have laid help upon one that is mighty," &c. Indeed, the whole scope of the psalm shows that it is so to be understood. Then, the "children" that are spoken of, are the spiritual children of the Saviour, true followers of the Lamb. And we can scarcely conceive how their security could be expressed in stronger language. Though they shall be chastised for their sins, yet his "loving kindness" will never be withdrawn, nor shall his "faithfulness fail."

I might here properly refer to a melancholy instance of the lengths to which errorists will go, to support a favourite theory. In the "Doctrinal Tracts" of the Methodist Church, page 212, the writer, in endeav uring to evade the force of so plain a statement of the doctrine of perseverance, says, that the covenant spoken of in this lxxxix. psalm, "relates wholly to David and his seed." He then misquotes the 35th verse. Instead of saying, "I will not lie unto David," he quotes it, "I will not fail David." And to crown all, he says, "God did also fail David." "He did alter the thing that had gone out of his lips, and yet without any impeachment of his truth. He abhorred and forsook his anointed. He did break the covenant of his servant," &c. The only reason he gives for saying that God broke his covenant is that it was conditional. That it was not conditional, in the sense which he affirms, I will not now stay to prove; for even if it were, it is still both false and impious to say, that "God broke his covenant, and altered the thing that had gone out of his lips." When a writer thus speaks of God, and misquotes his word, we need not be surprised at all his misrepresentations of Calvinism.

But let us see what Christ himself says on the doctrine of perseverance. Matt. xxiv. 24—"There shall arise false Christs, and false prophets, and shall show great signs and wonders; insomuch that, if it were possible, they shall deceive the very elect." John x. 27—29—"My sheep hear my voice, and I know them," (will he ever say he "never knew" them?) "and they follow me: and I give unto them eternal life; and they shall never perish, neither shall any man pluck them out of my hand. My Father, which gave them me, is greater than all; and no man is able to pluck them out of my Father's hand." Does not this look as if the Saviour meant to teach that believers are secure in the hands of God? But let us hear Paul. Rom. viii. 35—39 —"Who shall separate us from the love of Christ? Shall tribulation, or distress, or persecution, or famine, or nakedness, or peril, or sword? * * Nay, in all these things we are more than conquerors, through him that loved us. For I am persuaded, that neither death, nor life, nor angels, nor principalities, nor powers, nor things present, nor things to come, nor height, nor depth, nor any other creature, shall be able to separate us from the love of God, which is Christ Jesus our Lord." I cannot conceive how the doctrine could be stated in language more plain and forcible. I shall only add one passage more, though I might add scores. 1 Pet. i. 5—"Kept by the power of God, through faith, unto salvation." Here the whole doctrine of perseverance, through grace, faith, and holiness, is stated in a manner both concise and beautiful.

If we needed arguments from inference and supposition, we have them, too, in abundance. One, that seems to me incontrovertible, is drawn from the intercession of Christ. His prayer is—"Holy Father, keep through thine own name, those whom thou hast given me." Will the Father keep them, or deliver them over to Satan? We may leave the Arminian to answer.

Other inferential proofs, equally conclusive, might be given, but I think I have said enough to show you, that our Confession of Faith speaks the language of the Bible, and of common sense, when it says, chap. xvii. sec. 1—"They whom God hath accepted in his Beloved, effectually called and sanctified by his Spirit, can neither totally, nor finally, fall away from the state of grace, but shall certainly persevere therein to the end, and be eternally saved."

DIALOGUE XVII.

ADMISSION TO THE CHURCH.

Convert.—During the progress of our several conversations, on the different points of religious truth which we have considered, my mind has not only been relieved, but edified, and my desire to unite with some evangelical church has been increased. My preferences for the Presbyterian Church have also become stronger; but, still, with my limited knowledge, I do not know that I am prepared to say: "I sincerely receive and adopt the Confession of Faith, as containing the system of doctrines taught in the Holy Scriptures." My hesitancy does not arise from any opposition I have to any of its doctrines, but from my limited acquaintance with it. I have not, until recently, made it a study, and have not been able to compare it, in all its parts, with the Bible, so as to adopt it intelligently. And, I suppose, to adopt it "sincerely," means both a cordial and intelligent reception of all it teaches, as being in accordance with the Bible. And this, I have understood, you require of all your members.

Minister.—While you have had a misrepresentation of our doctrines, you have also had a false representation of our practice. I know it is common with those who wish to frighten young converts from joining our church, to tell them that they must have the Confession of Faith "crammed down their throats." But our form of government does not require it, nor have I ever known a single instance in which it has been required by any one of our church officers, that the members of the church should all adopt the Confession of Faith. It is required of all our church officers, but not of its members. It is not supposable, that all whom we might, in other respects, consistently receive to the church, are so well acquainted with all our doctrines, as to adopt them intelligently. Some who do not oppose them, are sometimes at a loss to understand them. It is common, in some sections of our church, to require those who unite with us, to receive and adopt the Confession of Faith, "as far as they are acquainted with it, and understand it;" but I have never known any one go further.

Con.—I could willingly and cheerfully do that, and cannot see any reasonable objection to such a course. But does the Confession of Faith contain no general requirement on the subject?

Min.—The "Directory for Worship," chap. 9, sec. 3, requires, that "those who are to be admitted to sealing ordinances shall be examined as to their knowledge and piety." And sec. 4 requires, that those who, when uniting with the church, receive the ordinance of baptism, shall, "in ordinary cases, make a public profession of their faith in the presence of the congregation." Thus, "knowledge and piety" are required of all, and a "public profession of their faith," of those who, at the time, receive the ordinance of baptism. How far the examination, as to knowledge and piety, shall be extended, and what may be comprised in the public profession of faith, required of others, is left to each church session, to decide according to circumstances. Thus, while piety and knowledge to some extent, are made indispensable requisites to membership in the Presbyterian Church, other things, though desirable, are not absolutely required. If a church session have satisfactory evidence that any one is a true child of God, and has knowledge of God and divine things, to such an extent, that he can profitably participate in the sealing ordinances of the church, it is all they require.

Con.—What is the common practice of church sessions in such cases?

Min.—The candidate for admission is examined on some of the leading points of Christian experience, upon which, any one who has the exercise of a true Christian, can easily give satisfaction. In connection with this, he is also examined on some of the leading doctrines of Christianity, especially, as connected with his experience. Thus, the ground of his hope is ascertained, and his faith in Christ is exhibited, which will qualify him for a member of the visible church; as, by regeneration and faith, he has been made a member of the body of Christ.

This course must commend itself to every reflecting mind, as the safest, both for the church and those who wish to become its members. A person cannot profitably participate in the sealing ordinances of the church, unless he have knowledge to discern the spiritual blessings which they represent. No one can rightly commemorate the Saviour, in the ordinance of the supper, if he have not faith and love. Neither would he make a suitable member of the church. All such members are an injury to the church, and their profession is an injury to themselves. To keep the church from being filled with such mem bers, the framers of our excellent formularies made piety and a certain degree of knowledge, prerequisites to membership. But this was going as far as they felt warranted by the word of God.

The General Assembly of our church speak particularly of this, in their pastoral letter of 1839: "The terms of Christian communion, adopted by our church, have been in accordance with the divine command, that we should receive one another as Christ has received us. We have ever admitted to our communion all those who, in the judgment of charity, were the sincere disciples of Jesus Christ. If, in some instances, stricter terms have been insisted upon—if candidates for sealing ordinances have been required to sign pledges, to make profession of anything more than faith, love, and obedience to Jesus Christ, these instances have been few and unauthorized, and, therefore, do not affect the general character of our church. We fully recognize the authority of the command, 'Him that is weak in the faith, receive ye, but not to doubtful disputations.' The application of this command, however, is entirely confined to private members of the church. It has no reference to the admission of men to offices in the church,"

&c. (Minutes of the General Assembly for 1839, p. 183.)

When such has always been the liberal policy of our church, you can perceive how much truth and honesty belong to those, who represent us as requiring all our members, to "swallow the Confession of Faith."

Con.—But what is the reason of the distinction made between the officers and members of the church?

Min.—The officers are entrusted with the management of all the concerns of the church; and it is a plain dictate of common sense, as well as of the Bible, that they should be men, who are not only well instructed in the doctrines of the church, but also cordially receive them. While the Bible commands us to stretch the broad wing of Christian charity over all who give evidence of being true disciples of Christ, and to receive them to our Christian fellowship, it is very pointed in its directions respecting the qualifications of all who bear rule in the house of God. They must not be "novices." They must "hold fast the form of sound words."—2 Tim. i. 13. "Holding fast the faithful word, as he hath been taught, that he may be able by sound doctrine, both to exhort and to convince the gainsayers."—Tit. i. 9. "Holding the mystery of the faith in a pure conscience."—1 Tim. iii. 9. This is in exact accordance with the requirement of our Confession, that all our officers should "sincerely receive and adopt" our form of sound words. I might mention many other passages bearing upon the same point, but it is not necessary, as the importance of having all our officers, cordially and intelligently, to embrace the same system of faith, will be obvious, when you look at their stations and duties. Our church, in some sections, for a time, pursued a different policy, but it had nearly proved her ruin.

Con.—But is true piety made an indispensable requisite, in all who wish to unite with the church?

Min.—So far as the true state of any one can be ascertained, it is. No one can search the heart, but there are some points in Christian experience, from which, in general, a correct judgment may be formed. And if, upon examination, any one gives satisfactory evidence, that he has not experienced a change of heart, he is uniformly rejected.

Con.—But would it not be better to receive every one who applies? Is not the prospect of conversion greater in the church, than out of it?

Min.—If the means of grace were accessible only to church members, there would be some reason for sinners to seek admission. But that is not the case. All the array of means of God's appointment, for the conversion of sinners, is intended for, and brought to bear upon, those who are out of the church. Indeed, when an unconverted sinner joins the church, he rather puts himself out of the way of many of those means of grace, which are intended for his benefit. Of what use, then, is a mere nominal connection with the church? A voluntary connection with the church, was by Christ and the apostles considered a profession of religion, and has been so ever since. Indeed, if it were not so, there would be no distinction between the church and the world. I need not stay to show you the great utility and importance of having the people of God united in a society, distinct and separate from the world. Anything that tends to break down this distinction, is ruinous in all its tendencies. And there is no better way to do it, than to have crowds of unconverted sinners gathered into the church. It is not only thus ruinous to the church, but it is injurious to the world, as it creates the impression, that a mere profession of religion is all that is necessary. The Presbyterian Church, for these reasons, has always made true piety an indispensable requisite, in all her members. I do not mean to say, that all her members are true disciples. We cannot, with all our care, judge the heart. We find that ministers and elders, even in the days of the apostles, were sometimes deceived in this matter; but it is always our aim to guard it as well as we can. We know that the higher we can raise the church above the world, the more clear and manifest we can make the distinction, the better it will be, both for the church and the world.

Con.—Your practice in this seems to me both wise and scriptural. It is certainly a happy reflection to any church member, that all his fellow-members have given satisfactory evidence to its officers, that they are true disciples of Christ. But there are some other denominations who pursue a different course. I have heard ministers proclaim from the pulpit, that the proper course was, "first to join the church, and then seek religion," that "the church was the best place to get religion," &c. And I myself, was often urged to join their church, when they knew, as well as myself, that I had no change of heart, but was fighting against God, in all his love.

Min.—I know that has become mournfully common. Many have been thus persuaded, that they will gain God's favour by insulting him. If the church be not a religious society, what is it? It is called the "household of the faithful, the body of Christ," &c. And for any one to unite with it, who does not belong to Christ, is making a false profession, and "lying both to God and man." It would be strange, indeed, if this were the way to secure the favour of the great Head of the Church.

The apostles pursued a very different course. They received to the church vast numbers, but we are told it was "of such as should be saved."—Acts ii. 47. And we know, that the character of the church for piety, stood so high, that it was a living reproof to the world. So much so, that we are told, Acts v. 13, that "of the rest durst no man join himself to them, but the people magnified them." What a commentary is this upon the practice of those who spend their zeal in gathering crowds of sinners, of all classes, into the church, seemingly more anxious that they should give their names to the church roll, than their hearts to God.

Con.—But would it not be better that, in the examination of candidates, for admission to the church, it should be conducted by the whole church, instead of its officers merely? The whole church would then not only have the benefit of the candidate's experience, if he be a true child of God, but it might be more satisfactory, also, that each member should hear and decide for himself.

Min.—In some particular and remarkable cases of conversion, it would, no doubt, be edifying and useful for all the members of the church to hear the candidate tell what God has done for him. But particular cases should never be made the ground of a general rule; and, I think, the experience of all churches who receive their members by a profession of their faith, as we do, will testify, that, as a general rule, it is more proper and expedient, to have it done by the officers of the church. But this involves one of the principal features of our form of church government, for which, we believe, we have scriptural authority and precedent. And a full and satisfactory consideration of this subject, would require more time than we can now devote to it. But if it would be gratifying to you, we will consider it at some future time.

Con.—I have never had any difficulty on the score of church government. The Presbyterian form has always struck me as wise and orderly, though my preferences for it are not the result of any examination of its principles. I would, therefore, be glad to embrace any opportunity of examining it more particularly.

Min.—Call when you have leisure, and I will endeavour to explain it to you, in the light of the Bible and of common sense.

DIALOGUE XVIII.

CHURCH GOVERNMENT.

Convert.—As I mentioned to you at our last interview, I have never thought much on the subject of church government, and have looked upon it as a matter of expediency merely; supposing there was no particular form authorized in the Bible, and consequently, it was left for the church to adopt any form of government, that according to circumstances might be deemed the most expedient.

Minister.—It is inconsistent with the Saviour's love to the church, and his care over her, to suppose, that in a matter affecting her interests so deeply, he would leave it entirely to the management of human wisdom. There are certain grand principles which the Bible gives for our direction, in all our duties toward our fellow-men, and especially as members of the church, in our duties to the church itself, and to each other individually. And in devising means for her peace, prosperity, and order, and labouring for her and our spiritual welfare, we surely cannot suppose that we are left without direction by our great and glorious Head. For this very purpose, we are told, that he instituted certain orders of men in the church, with peculiar offices and duties. Eph. iv. 11, 12—"He gave some apostles, and some prophets, and some evangelists, and some pastors and teachers, for the perfecting of the saints, for the work of the ministry, for the edifying of the body of Christ." 1 Cor. xii. 28—"God hath set some in the church, first apostles, secondarily prophets, thirdly teachers, after that miracles, then gifts of healing, helps, governments."

Con.—But some of these orders and gifts do not now exist, and may we not conclude that they were all only designed to continue for a time?

Min.—The extraordinary offices and gifts of those times are not now necessary, as the canon of revelation is complete; but as "pastors," or "teachers, helps, and governments," are still necessary for the church in every age, they are continued. But I mentioned those texts to show, that the officers of the church are of God's appointment. And I believe all evangelical denominations of Christians admit that some officers of the church, with peculiar duties, are divinely appointed, but all do not agree as to their number, rank, and duties, and the manner in which they should be appointed by the church, acting under the authority of her Head; and the difference of practice in these several particulars, constitutes the different forms of church government that now exist.

Con.—How many different forms of church government are there now found?

Min.—They may all be classed under four general heads, viz. Popery, Episcopacy, Independency, and Presbyterianism. There are, it is true, several varieties under each of these general kinds, but they all partake of the essential features of one or other, to such a degree, that they clearly belong to that class. For instance, the Episcopal and Methodist churches, though differing in some respects, both have all the essential features of Episcopacy, and are in fact Episcopal in their government. And on the other hand, Presbyterians, Reformed Presbyterians, Associate Presbyterians, and Associate-Reformed-Presbyterians, with the Dutch and German-Reformed churches, though they differ in some things as to church polity, all partake of the essential features of Presbyterianism, and are in fact Presbyterian in their government. There are also different shades of Independency or Congregationalism. some more and some less purely independent.

Con.—What are the grand, distinguishing features of Presbyterianism?

Min.—Presbyterianism is a spiritual republicanism—the grand distinctive feature of which is, power and authority invested in those who are chosen by the people, as their representatives or agents, to rule in their name. Thus it secures all the advantages of an aristocracy without any of its accompanying evils, and forms a union of all the different branches and sections of the government, more complete and binding than can be found in a monarchy, because it is a union by consent of the people, and ratified by them, in their capacity of members of the community. In Independency, there is no union which binds the different parts together, with any thing like a common feeling of interest. Each congregation is entirely independent of all others, and acting and living in its separate individual capacity, does not feel that it is an integral part of a common whole, bound by the same system of laws and regulations. Aristocracy and monarchy preserve a union of the different parts, but they deprive the people of their inalienable rights, of choosing their own rulers, &c. Republicanism, whilst it secures union, leaves the people in full possession of all their rights and liberties. It leaves all free, yet brings all under law. It places none above law, and leaves none below it.

Con.—But if the Presbyterian form of church government be thus based upon republican principles, how can it be said to be taken from the Bible? Republicanism is of recent date, as I believe our own government is the only one that has ever existed upon pure republican principles.

Min.—The close resemblance of our republican form of government to Presbyterianism, shows very clearly that they have the same origin, but it proves that true republicanism has its origin in Presbyterianism. Any one who traces their points of similarity, must be convinced that they have the same origin. Presbyterianism has its several official departments, legislative, judicial, and executive, with this difference from our civil government, that all these duties in our church government, belong to the same set of men. Every church court sits and acts in these several capacities, as circumstances require. And when any church court is about to sit in a judicial capacity, it is the duty of the Moderator, who is the presiding officer, to remind the body of "their high character as judges of a court of Jesus Christ, and the solemn duty in which they are about to act."—*General Rules for Judicatories*, 39. These duties, in our civil government, are vested in different bodies, but they all exactly correspond with our several church courts. Our church Session, as a judicial body, corresponds with our magistrate's court, the Presbytery with our County court, the Synod with our State court, and the General Assembly with our United States court. As a legislative body, the church Session corresponds with our township officers, called in some States trustees, and in others by different names. They meet, consult, devise measures, and make regulations for the general welfare of those who have chosen them to their office. The Presbytery corresponds with our board of County Commissioners, the Synod with our State Legislature, and the General Assembly with the Congress of the United States. With each body, also, from the lowest to the highest, are the several executive officers, with whom the similarity is equally striking.

Add to this, the grand principle of delegated power in a representative system, which forms the basis of both our civil and church governments, and the similarity is still more striking. Other points of similarity might be noticed, but this is sufficient to show any one, that one is modeled after the other, preserving all the grand features and outlines entire.

Con.—They must have had the same origin, but how do we know that Presbyterianism is the original, and republicanism the model?

Min.—From simple historical facts. We know that Presbyterianism existed, in all its purity, long before our government was thought of, and even before America was discovered. We know that it was persecution for Presbyterian principles, that drove our forefathers to this continent. For asserting their inalienable rights, and, in some instances, endeavouring to infuse republican principles into the governments of Europe, they were persecuted, and fled to this country, bringing their principles with them. They had learned them from the Bible, and prized them dearer than life. These principles formed the basis of all their colonial governments, and when they were infringed upon by the mother country, they maintained them with their blood. The same grand principles of civil and religious liberty, for which they were persecuted, and fled to this country, were those which appeared conspicuous in the contest, and for which they contended in the arduous struggle. When their liberties were achieved, and the several colonial governments formed one grand confederacy, the same principles were embodied in the federal constitution. And there they stand, giving us more consistent liberty, both civil and religious, than has ever been enjoyed by any nation under heaven, except, perhaps, that found in the theocracy of the Jews. The secret of our success as a republic is, that we have a government, whose principles are the republicanism of the Bible, which is only another name for Presbyterianism. To Presbyterianism, then, as derived from the Bible, we are indebted for our excellent form of government. The sound of liberty—civil and religious liberty—is delightful; but it is an exotic in this dark world, and we should never forget, that those principles, in the successful operation of which we rejoice, are drawn from the treasure of God's word, which gives to us, under all circumstances, perfect rules of life.

Con.—But where do we find in the Bible, any set of laws or regulations, designed for civil governments? The accounts we have of civil governments, are mostly of monarchies; and, in the New Testament times, Christians were subjects of the despotic governments then in existence. I was not aware that republicanism, in any shape, was taught in the Bible.

Min.—I know it is too generally thought that the Bible is adverse to human liberty. But I think I shall be able to show you, that the governments established by God, whether of Church or State, were all founded upon the same grand principles of Republicanism and Presbyterianism, which characterize ours. But as this investigation would require more time than we can devote to it at present, we will defer it until another time.

DIALOGUE XIX.

BIBLE REPUBLICANISM.

Convert.—Did I understand you as saying, at our last interview, that, according to Presbyterianism, all the authority and power of the officers of the church were derived from the people? You did not, I believe, say so in words, but I understood it as one of the principles of the system, that the power to rule must come from the people; and yet I cannot reconcile that with the Bible and the Confession of Faith, both of which acknowledge Christ as the fountain of all authority.

Minister.—The power and authority which belong to the office, are derived from Christ. All church officers hold their commission from him. But the authority to exercise that power, inherent in their respective offices, over any congregation, depends on the will of the people. If I am ordained a minister of the gospel, I have all the rights and privileges attached to that office, by the great Head of the church; but I have no authority over any congregation that does not choose me as their pastor, or that does not voluntarily subject itself to the Presbytery of which I am a member. The same is true of elders; and thus, ministers and elders, are the elected representatives of the people, the rulers whom they have voluntarily chosen. The people choose the persons whom they wish to bear rule over them, and then look to the Head of the church to clothe them with the authority requisite to constitute them their rulers. Thus, the authority of Christ, as Head of the church, and the grand principle of representation, are both acknowledged and preserved in perfect harmony. And in this too, you can see another point in which republicanism shows its Bible origin. The people, in a republican government, elect their officers, but they do not commission them, or induct them into office. That must be done by the proper authorities. Election is not considered as, in itself, vesting men with the peculiar rights and privileges belonging to the office to which they are elected. But when elected they are, by the constituted authorities of the government, clothed with the proper authority, to act as the representatives of those by whom they are elected and are invested with the rights and privileges belonging to their respective offices.

Con.—I perceive the resemblance is striking; but that our form of civil government is derived from the Bible, is a fact, I think, very little regarded, if known, or thought of at all, by the generality of men.

Min.—I know it is very little regarded, but still the facts are conclusive proof, that such is the case. The Bible gives us the first pattern of civil liberty and equality, that ever existed on republican principles. The pride and selfishness of man naturally tend to the extremes of power and wealth on the one hand, and oppression and poverty on the other. But that happy medium, where all are free and independent, yet all under law, none but God knew how to secure. And in the examples he has given us in his word, we have a light to guide us, which stands out as a beacon amid the dark conflicting elements of all other systems. I wish to direct your attention in the first place, very briefly, to the civil economy of the Jews, as established by God, when he brought them from Egyptian bondage, and gave them civil and religious freedom. The different tribes formed one grand confederacy, similar to ours, each one being sovereign in itself, for all the purposes of self-government. The doctrine of appeals, from the lower courts to the higher, is distinctly laid down; their highest court of appeal being the Sanhedrim, or seventy, corresponding to our federal court. The election of their rulers, was upon republican principles. Moses issues to them a proclamation: "Take ye wise men and understanding, and known among your tribes, and I will make them rulers over you," &c. That is, you elect, and I will commission, to their respective offices. Moses was their civil ruler, or president, first chosen by God himself, and afterwards by the common consent of the people. We do not read that there was a formal ratification of his appointment, as there was in the case of Joshua, his successor. We find them saying to Joshua, "All that thou commandest us, we will do. * * * According as we hearkened unto Moses, so will we hearken unto thee," &c. —Josh i. 16, 17. The power of their civil rulers was very limited; and they were distinctly told, that even if they should choose a king he must not consider himself in the light of a monarch. He must be chosen from among the people. He must not "multiply horses to himself." He must not "multiply to himself silver and gold," &c. He must be under the law equally with the rest. His heart must not be "lifted up above his brethren," &c.—Deut xvii. 16—20. Indeed, it is doubtful whether their constitution and government could have been so perfectly free, and yet efficient, had it not been that God himself was, for four hundred years, the supreme executive. When they desired a king, they were distinctly reproved for their folly, and warned of the encroachment on personal and public liberty, which would be the consequence. But even then, though, at their request, the executive authority was placed in the hands of a king, the republican form of government was not changed.

Con.—But how could a republican form of government exist under a king?

Min.—The person who was nominated for their king by God, was accepted by the people by acclamation; and though called a king, and invested with executive authority, was, in fact, nothing more at first, than commander-in-chief of a republic. His power and authority were limited, and regulated by a covenant or constitution, called "the manner of the kingdom," which was distinctly declared to the people; and, being ratified by them, was recorded in the statute book, and preserved as the palladium of their rights. "Samuel wrote it in a book, and laid it up before the Lord."—1 Sam. x. 25. We find the popular side of the government was so completely predominant, that even David did not dare openly to take the life of the lowest of his subjects, or even to punish offenders. When Uriah stood in his way, he had to resort to stratagem; and when Joab deserved death, he dare not execute it himself. "These sons of Zeruiah," he says, "are too hard for me." Their influence was so great, that he found it impossible to have them condemned by the proper authorities, without which he dare not proceed against them. These principles, however, were afterwards lost sight of, the people became corrupt, and their kings became despots; but for four hundred years, they enjoyed as much freedom in their government, as is consistent with efficiency, in any age that the world has yet seen, or probably will see.

Another excellent feature of this republican system, was the equal distribution of their land, by which every adult male was a landholder—the veritable owner of the soil on which he lived. There were no entailed estates, no hereditary nobility. Every family possessed its own land. This simple principle of ownership, in fee-simple, of the soil, is one of vast importance to a republican government. Indeed, it would seem to be one of its essential features. It encourages industry, inculcates patriotism, and is one of the main springs of civil liberty. Provision was made, in the laws given by God to Moses, for the perpetual preservation of this principle, so long as their constitution was held sacred. If, through misfortune, or other contingencies, any family was compelled to sell their land, it could not be alienated from the family longer than the year of jubilee. So that every fifty years the land reverted back to its original owners, in the regular line of descent. The law respecting the ownership of land, is very minutely laid down in the xxv. chapter of Leviticus, which, if you have never examined particularly, will amply repay you for an attentive perusal. It shows divine wisdom, in its excellent provisions. A man by carelessness, or wickedness, might deprive himself of all the benefits arising from ownership in land; but no vice, or slothfulness, or misfortune, could deprive his family of their portion of the soil.

In the setting apart of the tribe of Levi as public instructors, there was provision made for a general system of education, which resulted most happily, in raising the whole mass of the people, to a degree of refinement and intelligence, then not equalled in the world.

Con.—But where do we find, in the laws given by God to Moses, anything like a civil constitution, or a system of laws expressly designed for their civil economy?

Min.—In those laws we find three classes. First, those which are called moral, which are obligatory on all men, under all circumstances, universally and perpetually. Second, those which are called ceremonial, which prescribe the rites and forms of the Jewish worship. Third, those which are called judicial, which relate entirely to their civil economy, and in which we find all the principles which I have mentioned as the prominent features of republicanism, standing out conspicuously. They preserve, in the hands of the people, as much personal liberty as ever was, or perhaps can be, combined with a permanent and efficient national government. These laws, moreover, were formally adopted by the people. When Moses rehearsed to them the words of God, they answered with one unanimous voice—"All the words which the Lord hath said, we will do." Thus their laws, their civil constitution, were accepted and adopted. This adoption of their constitution, was repeated at the death of Moses; and, by a statute, ever after, from generation to generation, once in seven years, the tribes were required to meet in a great national convention, solemnly to ratify their constitution.

From this very brief view of the Jewish government, you may see the origin of those principles of civil and religious liberty, which prove so rich a blessing wherever adopted, and fairly carried out.

Con.—But is there any proof that their ecclesiastical affairs were conducted upon the same principles?

Min.—I have before remarked, that for four hundred years, in the theocracy of the Jews, God himself was the supreme executive. Consequently, their civil and ecclesiastical polities were blended, to a considerable extent, in one system. Their several courts seem to have had the adjudication of all matters, both civil and religious. This was necessary, considering the circumstances under which the Jewish government was instituted and existed. It seems to have been the object of God, in establishing the Mosaic economy, to fortify his people against idolatry, and preserve a pure religion, as well as to stop the march of despotism, lust and blood, which darkened and cursed the whole world besides. The nations of the earth had cast off his allegiance, and turned their back upon him, and his commandments. He chose for himself a nation to whom he committed his word and his worship, and who, as a pattern of excellence in all respects, might exhibit to an apostate world the "blessedness of that nation whose God is the Lord." It was, therefore, necessary, that God should appear conspicuous as their immediate lawgiver and executive, in all that pertained to their welfare, both civil and religious. The blessed effects of true religion upon a national government, were also to be exhibited, and, consequently, we find their civil and ecclesiastical polities blended in one system. Even their great national convention, at which they deliberated upon, and, if necessary, modified their constitution and laws, was called "an holy convocation." Their church government, therefore, partook of the same features which characterized their civil government, and here we find Presbyterianism in all its essential features. But as on this point I wish to be a little more specific, we will take some other opportunity to consider it more at length, than our time at present will permit.

DIALOGUE XX.

BIBLE PRESBYTERIANISM.

Convert.—Since our last conversation, I have been examining, to some extent, the account we have in the Bible respecting the government of the Jews, as established by Moses, according to the direction of God, and find very frequent mention made of "Elders," who seem to have been officers or rulers among them. Is it from that title and office, that the office and title of "Ruling Elder" of the Presbyterian system are derived?

Minister.—The term Elder literally signifies an aged person. The word in the original languages of the Bible has the same signification. Persons of age and experience were usually selected to fill stations of honour and trust, because of their gravity and wisdom; consequently, the term Elder became an established title of office. The titles of Alderman, Senator, and others, are of the same origin. The term Presbyter is simply the Greek word for Elder, transferred into our language with a slight change in its orthography, without being translated.

The office of Elder is derived from that which the title signified with the "Elders of Israel," that is, the elders of the Presbyterian Church hold a similar station, with similar duties and obligations. The "Elders of Israel" seem to have been the acknowledged representatives of the people, acting for them, and in their name. Even during their bondage in Egypt, they seem to have had those who were termed Elders officially, who acted by authority in behalf of the people. God said to Moses, Ex. iii. 16—"Go and gather the Elders of Israel together, and say unto them," &c. Here was a message that concerned the whole mass of the people, and no doubt was designed for them; yet Moses was commanded not to deliver it to the people themselves, but to their representatives, the Elders, whose duty it would consequently be, to make it known to the people. Moses was also commanded to take with him "the Elders of Israel," when he should go with the message of God to Pharaoh, (Ex. iii. 18,) that he might see that it was the voice of the whole congregation of Israel speaking through their Elders. Moses himself was not counted sufficient, which shows they had no aristocracy; the people were not required to attend, which is contrary to independency; but the Elders of the people were called, to whom it was committed.

Con.—But we read frequently, that God told Moses to "speak unto the children of Israel;" from which it would seem, that the people themselves were most generally appealed to.

Min.—In such cases, we are to understand the direction of God to Moses, to be in accordance with their established usage. He had, in the first instance, named the Elders particularly, as those through whom Moses should communicate to the people his messages; and, consequently, it is to be understood, that when God tells him to "speak unto the children of Israel," he meant that he should communicate with them through the same channel. This is plain from the fact, that it would be impossible for Moses to deliver his messages to the whole congregation of the people. It was impossible, in their circumstances, to assemble the whole multitude; and, if assembled, he could not speak to them all. It is, therefore, most natural to suppose, that it was always done through the Elders, especially, seeing that they are so frequently mentioned as those through whom

God and Moses communicated with the people. In Ex. xvii. 5, 6, the Elders were selected to witness the miracle of striking the rock in Horeb. We find them, also, on other occasions, selected for similar purposes.—Ex. xxiv. 1, 9.

The principle of representation is very strikingly exhibited in Lev. iv. 13—15—"If the whole congregation sin," &c., "the Elders of the congregation shall lay their hands upon the head of the bullock," brought for a sin offering. Here it is plain, that the Elders were viewed as representing the whole congregation; and what they did in the name of the congregation, was accepted by God as the act of the whole.

In many instances during the journeyings of the Israelites through the wilderness, the Elders are spoken of as being called together by Moses, to deliberate on important matters, or to receive communications for the people. The following passages you may note down and consult at your leisure—Ex. xviii. 12; Numb. xi. 16, 25; Deut. xxv. 7; xxix. 10; xxxi. 28; xxxiii. 7; Josh. xxiv. 31. In these and many other passages, you will find Elders spoken of in their official capacity, as acting authoritatively for, and in behalf of the people. Their care over the morality and religion of the people, and the beneficial effects of their supervision, are spoken of in Josh. xxiv. 31—"Israel served the Lord all the days of Joshua, and of the Elders that overlived Joshua, and which had known all the works of the Lord that he had done for Israel." The frequent mention made of them through the whole period of the Jewish history, shows very clearly, that even in their lowest condition, they did not lose sight entirely of the principles upon which their government was first established.

Con.—But when their civil government was changed under their kings, would it not also have the effect of changing, or modifying, their system of church government, seeing that they were so intimately connected in their first establishment?

Min.—To what extent their civil government became changed, it is difficult to ascertain. It was more or less despotic under their different kings, in proportion as each one was disposed to regard his duty to God and man. Still, however, we find some traces of republicanism, in the darkest periods of their history. But as the civil government became changed, the church seems to have separated from it. We find in the synagogue service and order, a system of church government entirely distinct and separate, comprising in itself a complete system of church polity. It is, indeed, contended by some very able biblical scholars, that this distinction between the civil and ecclesiastical polities of the Jews, existed from the first setting up of the tabernacle in the wilderness. There can be no doubt, however, that it existed afterwards in the order and service of their synagogues.

Con.—When was the synagogue service first established?

Min.—It perhaps cannot be clearly ascertained. Philo, in his life of Moses, gives some good reasons for the opinion that it was instituted by him. Dr. Prideaux contends, that it could not have existed previous to the return of the Jews from their captivity in Babylon. His reasoning, however, is not conclusive. He founds his opinion mainly upon the fact, that the reading and expounding of the Scriptures then extant, was the most prominent of synagogue services, and as copies of the Scriptures were not generally distributed previous to the captivity, the synagogue service, he thinks, could not have existed. The other services of the synagogue, however, praise, prayer, and exhortation, might have existed previously; and, after the captivity, reading and expounding the law may have been added. It does not appear that the Jews were at any time restricted to any particular place for the performance of their devotional exercises, though their sacrifices could only be offered at the tabernacle, or temple. We know that praise and prayer were offered, and instruction given, at the "schools of the prophets," of which we find mention made as early as the days of Samuel. How long before Samuel they were instituted, cannot be clearly ascertained. The devout Israelites were in the habit of assembling at these schools, for the purposes of devotion and instruction, on their new moons and Sabbaths. 1 Sam. x. 5—11; xix. 18—24. 2 Kings iv. 23. The natural course would be, that these places for meeting would be multiplied, as the wants of the people seemed to demand, and a regular order of conducting divine worship would be introduced. In Ezek. xiv. 1, and xx. 1, compared with Neh. viii. 17, 18, we have intimations that such was the case. In Psa. lxxxiv. there seems to be a direct allusion to such places of worship; and, in Psa. lxxiv. 8, the Psalmist, speaking of the desolations wrought by their enemies, says expressly, "They have burnt up all the synagogues of God in the land."

The most natural conclusion, therefore

is, as it seems to me, that the prophets and holy men—"the Elders of Israel"—under the direction of God, instituted the synagogue service at a very early period, first by devout assemblies at the schools of the prophets, and the houses of holy men; and these domestic congregations being multiplied, as the wants of the people seemed to demand, and becoming fixed in certain places, a distinct system of church polity, and a regular order of conducting divine service, was introduced. This point, however, is not of much importance to our present inquiry. We know that there was such a system in existence when our Saviour came upon earth; and that when the Christian church was set up as a regular organization by the apostles, they adopted the order of the synagogue.

Con.—But was that Presbyterianism?

Min.—In every synagogue there was a bench of Elders, consisting of three or more persons, who were entrusted with its whole government and discipline. The synagogues were the parish or district churches of the Jews, in which the Elders, as a court, or bench of rulers, received members, judged, censured, and excluded, or excommunicated. Their sentence of excommunication was termed "putting him out of the synagogue"—John ix. 22, and xii. 42—and the Elders were called "the rulers of the synagogue," of whom we have frequent mention in the New Testament. We find, therefore, that in the synagogues, all the essential principles of Presbyterianism were universally established. The similarity in every important point was exact. We find, also, that in addition to this bench of Elders in each synagogue, there was one principal overseer, who was called the "Bishop," or "Angel of the church," who was the presiding officer, or Moderator. From these lower courts, also, there was an appeal to the "great synagogue" at Jerusalem; thus blending the whole community together as one visible professing body.

In this, I believe, all commentators and biblical scholars agree, be their prepossessions as to church government what they may. Did time permit, I could quote to you Stillingfleet, Vitringa, Selden, Grotius, Lightfoot, Thorndike, Burnet, Godwin, Neander, Spencer, and others, who all agree, in every important point, respecting the order and polity of the synagogue. The testimony of these eminent men is rendered more conclusive from the fact, that they were not Presbyterians, with, perhaps, one or two exceptions. I might also quote Dr. Gill, and Dr. Adam Clarke, as teaching the same truth. The extensive learning and deep research of these eminent men, no competent judge will call in question; and as one was a Baptist and the other a Methodist, they cannot be accused of favouring Presbyterianism, further than in giving what they conceived to be the plain sense of the Scriptures.

The first converts to Christianity were mostly native Jews, and as they had been accustomed to the exercise of church government in the manner specified, entirely distinct from the temple worship, which was ceremonial and typical, it is not surprising that it should be adopted by the apostles in the organization of the primitive church. That this was the case, we have abundant evidence, which is so conclusive that it seems to me a matter of wonder that it should be controverted. At a future time, I will give you a brief summary of the evidence that the primitive church was truly Presbyterian, and continued so until it was corrupted by Popery, which will, I think, convince you of the Scriptural warrant for Presbyterianism.

DIALOGUE XXI.

PRIMITIVE PRESBYTERIANISM.

Convert.—A difficulty has occurred to my mind since our last conversation, respecting the officers of the synagogue. You spoke of Elders, but I do not recollect that you said anything about Ministers, as belonging to the established order of the synagogue, unless the presiding officer, "the Angel of the church," acted in that capacity.

Minister.—It was one of the duties of the chief rulers of the synagogue, to teach the people from the Scriptures. This they did sometimes by way of conference, or questions and answers, and sometimes by continued discourses, like sermons. These different ways of teaching they called by the general name of searching, and the discourse was called a search, or inquiry. The chief ruler or president also invited others, whom he thought capable, to speak in the synagogue; and that honour was generally offered to strangers, if any were present, who were thought to have the gift of speaking.—Luke iv. 16—22; Acts

21

xiii. 14, 15. These presidents, or chief rulers, together with the bench of Elders, were called rulers. Hence, in the primitive church, the preacher or pastor, together with the bench of Elders, were called by the general name of Elders. Paul, in giving instruction to Timothy, tells him, "Let the Elders that rule well, be counted worthy of double honour, especially they who labour in the word and doctrine."—1 Tim. v. 17. From which it is plain, that there was a class of Elders, who did not labour in word and doctrine. Peter called himself an Elder, and we know he was a preacher. We know, also, that there were Elders who ruled, yet did not preach, because there was a plurality of them ordained in every church, however small, and we cannot suppose that in every church they had a plurality of pastors.

Con.—But how do we know that these Pastors and Elders sustained the same office, and were clothed with the same authority, which we now find invested in the officers of the Presbyterian Church?

Min.—We find the Elders represented as "overseers" of the church. "Take heed therefore unto yourselves, and to all the flock over the which the Holy Ghost hath made you overseers."—Acts xx. 28. They are also called rulers. "Let the Elders that rule well."—1 Tim. v. 17: "Obey them that have the rule over you," &c.—Heb. xiii. 17. The people, too, are exhorted to obey them, to submit to them, &c., as to persons charged with an oversight of their spiritual interests. "And we beseech you, brethren, to know them which labour among you, and are over you in the Lord, and admonish you; and to esteem them very highly in love for their work's sake.—1 Thess. v. 12, 13. "Obey them that have the rule over you, and submit yourselves," &c.—Heb. xiii. 17. Now, when we find a plurality of Elders ordained in every church, and one of these Elders "labouring in word and doctrine," and others not; and when we find that the people were exhorted to obey them, and submit to them in the Lord; and, also, that these Elders were chosen by the people, and ordained to their office by the laying on of hands; we have all the essential principles of Presbyterianism. This will appear to you the more plain, when you recur to the fact I before noticed, that the term Presbyter is the same with Elder. In the one case it is translated, and in the other it is simply transferred, with a slight change in orthography.

Con.—But we find the word Bishop often used to denote an office then existing in the church, and does not this fact afford some ground for Episcopacy?

Min.—The term "Bishop," like that of Presbyter, is transferred into our language without being translated. It means an overseer, and we have it so translated in several instances. "Take heed to yourselves, and to all the flock over the which the Holy Ghost hath made you overseers," (or Bishops.)—Acts xx. 28. The Elders are styled Bishops, as they have the oversight of the flock, and the terms Bishop, and Elder, are titles given interchangeably to the same persons, which plainly shows that the term Bishop was no more than the title which designated the pastor, or overseer of a single church. We do not find in the New Testament a single trace of Episcopacy, in its modern form. Indeed, the placing of one minister above another is expressly forbidden. There is but one commission given by the Lord Jesus Christ to his ministers: "Go and teach all nations, baptizing them in the name of the Father, and of the Son, and of the Holy Ghost." And anything like one minister being placed higher in authority than the rest, and having rule over them, and possessing alone the power of ordination, is directly in the face of the commands of Christ, and all the instituted order of the primitive church. There is not a solitary instance in all the New Testament, of an ordination being performed by a single individual, but the power is uniformly represented as being possessed, and exercised, by the ordinary pastors, and performed by the "laying on of the hands of the Presbytery."—1 Tim. iv. 14; Acts xiii. 3; which corresponds with Presbyterianism, and with Presbyterianism alone. That this was the form of church government adopted by the apostles, and left in universal use when these inspired men left the church to their successors, it really seems almost impossible that any impartial and candid reader of the New Testament can entertain a doubt.

Con.—But have we also authority, or precedent, for the several church courts which we find in use in the Presbyterian church?

Min.—It is very plain, that the whole church, as it then existed, however scattered, was regarded as one body, all governed by the same laws, and subject to the same authority. When a subject of importance arose, about which there was diversity of opinion, we find the matter considered and decided by a synod composed of the "apostles and elders."—Acts xv. We have in this chapter an account of the doings of the Synod, which met at Jerusalem, and have it particularly stated, that their decision respecting the overture which was brought before them, was sent down to "all the churches," carrying with it the authority of the Synod for their regulation. We find, also, that this decree with others, was recorded and delivered to the churches, to be registered, preserved, and obeyed. As Paul and Timothy "went through the cities, they delivered them the decrees for to keep, which were ordained by the apostles and elders which were at Jerusalem."—Acts xvi. 4. Here, then, we find an assembly of ministers and elders acting as the representatives of the whole church, and pronouncing authoritative decisions, which were intended to bind the whole body. If this be not Presbyterianism, we will search for it in vain, either in Scotland or America.

Con.—How long did the church continue under Presbyterian government, and what was the cause of the change?

Min.—It is difficult to ascertain precisely the time of the first departure from Presbyterianism. The change was, no doubt, small at first, and thought to be trivial. Clemens Romanus, an eminent Father, who lived near the close of the first century, in a letter directed to the Christians at Corinth, chides them for having, at the instigation of a few leading men, departed, in one respect, from the wise and wholesome system of church government established by the apostles. "It is a shame," he writes, "yea, a very great shame, to hear that the most firm and ancient church of the Corinthians should be led, by one or two persons, to rise up against their Elders. * * * Let the flock of Christ enjoy peace, with the Elders that are set over them. * * * Do ye, therefore, who first laid the foundation for this sedition, submit yourselves to your Elders." Two things are plain from these expressions. First, that the Corinthian church had been organized upon Presbyterian principles, and had so continued for a time, probably during one generation. Second, that a departure from it was viewed by this eminent Father as deserving of censure. This, however, was only a solitary case, and the defection did not become general for a length of time afterwards. But it shows how prone men are to depart from the simplicity of the order of the primitive times. The testimony of the Fathers is abundant and clear, that the church, in general, continued to enjoy the primitive Presbyterian form of government for at least two centuries. Did time permit, I might quote to you, Ignatius, Polycarp, Irenæus, Cyprian, Origen, Ambrose, Augustine, Justin Martyr, and others, as stating the same truths, that in the early ages of the church, the different, distinct churches were under the care of a Bishop, or Pastor, and a bench of Elders, and that there was no priority, or pre-eminence of rank among the ministers. Indeed, for the first two hundred years after Christ, we find no traces of either Prelacy or Independency, except they may be traced in the few departures from Presbyterianism, which we find condemned and censured by the Fathers. Ambrose, who lived in the fourth century, in his commentary on 1 Tim. v. 1, says, that "the synagogues, and afterwards the church, had Elders, without whose counsel nothing was done in the church, which grew into disuse, by what negligence, I know not, unless, perhaps, by the sloth, or rather the pride, of the Teachers, while they alone, wished to appear something." That there were Elders and Teachers, as distinct classes of officers in the primitive church, Ambrose asserts positively, and expresses his opinion, that they "grew into disuse, from the sloth or pride of the teachers." We find from the history of those times, that both the Ministry and Eldership of the church, declined in zeal and faithfulness. The pictures given of the cupidity, mutual encroachments and strife of the clergy, even in the third century, by Cyprian, Origen, and Eusebius, are truly mournful. In such a state of things it is not surprising, that the simplicity of the primitive church gave place to a system which flattered ambition, and fed voluptuousness. Among such ministers, a grasping after preferment, titles, &c., might be confidently expected. The pastors in the large cities, and more opulent towns, began to claim a pre-eminence and peculiar powers, which by little and little were admitted, and at length established, as a part of the order of Christ's house. And, finally, the bishops became "lords over God's heritage," rather than "ensamples to the flock;" and to crown all, one was proclaimed "universal Bishop," under the title of Pope—declared to be the "Vicar of God,"—with universal, unlimited authority over the souls and bodies of all men in the world.

Con.—And was the primitive order of the church so entirely lost in this universal corruption, that none remained to bear witness to the truth?

Min.—The Paulicians we find, in the seventh century, testifying against the encroachments of Prelacy, and afterwards the Waldenses and Albigenses, still more distinctly and zealously, protested against the errors of the times, and especially, the encroachments on Presbyterian simplicity. It was, indeed, supposed that the Waldenses were prior to the Paulicians. The noted Reinerius, who lived near three hundred years before Luther, and had once resided with the Waldenses, though he afterwards became one of their bitterest persecutors, in a treatise he wrote against them, ascribes to them a very early origin. He said they were "the most pernicious to the Church of Rome of all other heretics, for three reasons. First, because they were older than any other sect, for some say they have been ever since Pope Sylvester, (A. D. 314,) and others say from the time of the apostles." Their origin is too remote to be traced with distinctness and certainty. That they were Presbyterian both in doctrine and order, must be admitted by all. John Paul Perrin, their historian, who was one of their ministers, speaks particularly of their Elders and Pastors, as distinct classes of officers in the church, and represents their Synods as composed of Ministers and Elders. Gilly, another historian of the Waldenses, quotes their Confession of Faith, as containing the following declaration: "It is necessary for the church to have Pastors, to preach God's word, to administer the sacraments, and to watch over the sheep of Jesus Christ; and also Elders and Deacons, according to the rules of good and holy church discipline, and the practice of the primitive church." This not only shows beyond doubt that the Waldenses were Presbyterians, but it also shows what they believed respecting the Presbyterianism of the primitive church. Other historians of undisputed authority, assert the same respecting the Waldenses, and the Bohemians, and the Albigenses, who were different branches of the same people, and called by different names, as they lived at different times, and in different places. Moreland, Ranken, Comenius, Bucer, and others, all give decisive testimony to the fact, that these witnesses for the truth, during the long period of darkness and corruption which overspread the church, were decidedly Presbyterian, both in doctrine and order.*

Thus I have endeavoured to give you a very brief and hasty view of Presbyterianism from the days of the apostles to the reformation by Luther. To the facts that

* See a very interesting "History of the Waldenses," illustrated with beautiful engravings, published by the Board of Publication.

I have stated, volumes of testimony might be given, but circumstances would only permit us to glance at a small part of it. But from what has been said, you can perceive the puerile ignorance manifested by those who allege that Presbyterianism was invented by Calvin.

Con.—Were the Reformers Presbyterian in their sentiments and practice?

Min.—All the Reformers, of any note, agreed upon all the essential principles of Presbyterianism. But as our conversation has been sufficiently protracted at this time, we will on some future occasion examine what history says on that point.

DIALOGUE XXII.

PRESBYTERIANISM OF THE REFORMERS.

Convert.—In our former conversations I have not noticed, that among the officers of the Presbyterian church, you said anything respecting Deacons, yet they are frequently mentioned in the New Testament; and I find, also, mention made of them in the Confession of the Waldenses. They are also, I believe, in most Presbyterian churches that I am acquainted with.

Minister.—The office of Deacon is a very important one, and should be found in every church, where circumstances require and admit of it; still, however, it is not an essential part of Presbyterianism, that is, a church may exist, and act upon Presbyterian principles, in which they are not found. The want of this office does not destroy its Presbyterianism; whereas, a Presbyterian church cannot exist without Elders. Deacons existed in the synagogues, and were afterwards introduced by the apostles into the primitive church, as soon as circumstances seemed to require it.

We find that the church had existed for some time, and when "the number of disciples was multiplied," circumstances seemed to call for the appointment of some, whose special business it should be to attend to the temporal concerns of the church, especially to superintend her benevolent operations.—Acts vi. So in every church in which this part of its business requires much of the attention of the minister and elders, if the circumstances at all admit of it, they should have "Deacons set over the work," who should be solemnly ordained by prayer and the laying on of hands, in the same way that the other officers are ordained. The importance of the office to the church you can easily perceive, and it shows in a very clear light the wisdom of the Great Head of the church, in arranging all things necessary to her peace, comfort and prosperity. Hence, we find, that though the office of Deacon has not been uniformly found in all Presbyterian churches, yet it has been generally contended for by those, who seek entire conformity to the order of the primitive church.

Con.—Was Calvin the first of the Reformers who sought to establish Presbyterianism according to the order of the primitive church? I have thought, that perhaps this gave rise to the idea, that he originated it. If he was the first of the Reformers who adopted it, the more ignorant might conclude that it originated with him.

Min.—The allegation that Presbyterianism originated with Calvin, has not even that foundation. Ulric Zuingle, the leader of the Reformation in Switzerland, who lived long before Calvin, and died before ever Calvin saw Geneva, or had appeared among the prominent Reformers, thus speaks on the subject of Ruling Elders: "The title of Presbyter, or Elder, as used in Scripture, is not rightly understood by those, who consider it as applicable only to those who preside in preaching: for it is evident, that the term is also sometimes used to designate Elders of another kind, that is, Senators, Leaders, or Counsellors."

Œcolampadius, whom D'Aubigné in his history mentions as one of the bright stars of the Reformation, and who was contemporary with Luther, but died before Calvin came on the stage of action, thus speaks of Ruling Elders: "But it is evident, that those which are here intended, are certain Seniors or Elders, such as were in the apostles' days, and who of old time were called *Presbuteroi*, whose judgment, being that of the most prudent part of the church, was considered as the decision of the whole church." The testimony of Bucer, Lasco, Peter Martyr, and others, is equally clear as to the fact, that Presbyterianism was one of the grand principles of the Reformation. Luther, himself, in speaking of the Bohemian church, says: "There hath not arisen any people since the times of the apostles, whose church hath come nearer to the apostolic doctrine and order, than the brethren of Bohemia. * * * In the ordinary discipline of the church they use, and whereby they happily govern the churches, they go far beyond us, and are in this respect far more praiseworthy." Now, in view of the fact before stated, that the Bohemian Church was strictly Presbyterian, the sentiments of Luther are plain. Melancthon, Farel, Viret and others might be added to the list of eminent Reformers, who all agree on the great principles of Presbyterianism, viz: equality of rank among ministers, and the government of the church by Ministers and Elders.

Calvin, when he first settled at Geneva, found the church there in great need of discipline, and for attempting to establish a system that would exclude gross offenders from the sealing ordinances of the church, he was banished from the city and retired to Strasburg. While there, feeling the great want of some regular system of church discipline, he opened a correspondence with some of the principal men of the Bohemian church. Comenius, in his history of the Bohemians, gives some extracts from some of his letters, in which he speaks in high terms of their form of church government, as being not only wise and wholesome, but also in accordance with the apostolic order. Near four years afterwards he was recalled to Geneva, and made it one of the conditions of his accepting the pastoral charge of the church, that he should be permitted to have a bench of Elders, to conduct the discipline of the church, according to the plan in use among the Bohemians. Thus, Presbyterianism was established in Geneva, and became general in the Reformed Churches in Switzerland, Germany, Holland, France, Hungary, Scotland, and throughout Europe generally, with the exception of England.

Con.—Why was it not received and adopted in England?

Min.—In the reformation from Popery in England, the kings and bishops mostly took the lead. To them, as a matter of course, the simple republicanism of the Presbyterian system would not be agreea-

22*

ble. Ecclesiastical pre-eminence had long been established, and it is not surprising that they should wish to retain it. Accordingly, while they adopted the system of doctrine taught by the Reformers generally, they retained many of the features of Popery in their system of church government. This, however, was contrary to the expressed opinion of many of their most learned and pious divines. Not a few of the brightest stars of the Church of England have given their decided opinion in favour of Presbyterianism. The truly venerable and pious Dr. Owen, gives his opinion on 1 Tim. v. 17, in the following unequivocal language: "This is a text of uncontrollable evidence, if it had anything to conflict withal, but prejudice and interest. A rational man, who is unprejudiced, who never heard of the controversy about Ruling Elders, can hardly avoid an apprehension, that there were two sorts of Elders, some who labour in the word and doctrine, and some who do not so do. The truth is, it was interest and prejudice which first caused some learned men to strain their wits to find out evasions from the evidence of this testimony. Being found out, some others of meaner abilities have been entangled by them. * * * There are, then, Elders in the church. There are, or ought to be so, in every church. With these Elders the whole rule of the church is entrusted. All these, and only they, do rule in it." This, from an Independent divine of so much eminence and piety as Dr. Owen, is as strong human testimony in favour of Presbyterianism, as any one can wish. Dr. Whitely bears the same testimony, in language equally plain. Thorndike, Whitaker, and others, clearly express the same opinion; and even Archbishop Cranmer, once proposed the introduction of Ruling Elders into the Church of England. From all this testimony it is plain, that though Prelacy was established in the national church, many of her most eminent men were in favour of Presbyterianism, as being in accordance with apostolic order. I have purposely avoided quoting the opinions of Presbyterians, because they might be considered partial to their own system. But when we find the system supported by the arguments of Episcopalians and Independents, partiality to Presbyterianism cannot be alleged. I might add testimony, equally plain, from many others, both Episcopalians and Independents, but I think I have said enough to convince you, that the order of the Presbyterian church, as well as her doctrine, is in accordance with the Bible and common sense, and has received the suffrages of the wise and good in every age. Did time permit, it would be a pleasant task to trace with you the history of the Presbyterian church more at large. Millions of her martyrs have sealed the truth of her doctrines with their blood; and though persecuted in every age, she still lives, and witnesses for the truth. But for this I must refer you to history.

THE END.

www.ingramcontent.com/pod-product-compliance
Lightning Source LLC
LaVergne TN
LVHW010252110826
845151LV00004B/1454

* 9 7 8 1 4 2 5 5 2 3 4 3 5 *